# *Library Blogging*

## *Karen A. Coombs*
## *and Jason Griffey*

Professional Development Resources for
K-12 Library Media and Technology Specialists

# Dedications

*Karen A. Coombs* - To my grandmother Tsetsilas for helping me to explore the world, believe in myself, and have big dreams; and to Michael for being the most patient husband in the world, taking me on a writing retreat, and keeping domestic stuff from coming apart while I obsessed and wrote.

*Jason Griffey* – This book is dedicated to Betsy, who never doubts me; to Eliza, who I loved before meeting, and doubly after; to my Mom and Dad, for giving me the opportunity to sit in my room with my Commodore 64 when I was 12; to my coworkers at UTC for putting up with me during the writing process; and to all my friends, virtual and real, who made me who I am. I am indebted to you all.

Library of Congress Cataloging-in-Publication Data

Coombs, Karen A.
  Library blogging / Karen A. Coombs and Jason Griffey.
    p. cm.
  Includes index.
  ISBN-13: 978-1-58683-331-2 (pbk.)
  ISBN-10: 1-58683-331-6 (pbk.)
  1. Communication in library science--Technological innovations. 2. Library science--Blogs. 3. Librarians--Blogs. 4. Blogs. 5. Library Web sites--Design. I. Griffey, Jason. II. Title.
  Z680.3C66 2008
  006.7--dc22
                              2008013786

Cynthia Anderson: Editor
Carol Simpson: Editorial Director
Judi Repman: Consulting Editor

Published by Linworth Publishing, Inc.
3650 Olentangy River Road
Suite 250
Columbus, Ohio 43214

ISBN 13: 978-1-58683-331-2
ISBN 10: 1-58683-331-6


5 4 3 2 1

# TABLE *of* CONTENTS

Dedications . . . . . . . . . . . . . . . . . . . . . . . . . . . . . . . . . . . . . . . . . . . . . . . . . . .ii
Table of Contents . . . . . . . . . . . . . . . . . . . . . . . . . . . . . . . . . . . . . . . . . . . . .iii
Table of Figures . . . . . . . . . . . . . . . . . . . . . . . . . . . . . . . . . . . . . . . . . . . . . . .v
About the Authors . . . . . . . . . . . . . . . . . . . . . . . . . . . . . . . . . . . . . . . . . . . .ix
Introduction . . . . . . . . . . . . . . . . . . . . . . . . . . . . . . . . . . . . . . . . . . . . . . . . . .x

**CHAPTER 1: An Introduction to Blogs** . . . . . . . . . . . . . . . . . . . . . . . . .1
  What is a Blog? . . . . . . . . . . . . . . . . . . . . . . . . . . . . . . . . . . . . . . . . . . . . .1
  History of Blogging . . . . . . . . . . . . . . . . . . . . . . . . . . . . . . . . . . . . . . . . .4
  Why Blog? . . . . . . . . . . . . . . . . . . . . . . . . . . . . . . . . . . . . . . . . . . . . . . . . .7
  Sociology of Blogging . . . . . . . . . . . . . . . . . . . . . . . . . . . . . . . . . . . . . . .8

**CHAPTER 2: Why a Library Blog?** . . . . . . . . . . . . . . . . . . . . . . . . . . . .11
  Blog as News Portal . . . . . . . . . . . . . . . . . . . . . . . . . . . . . . . . . . . . . . . .12
  Internal Communication . . . . . . . . . . . . . . . . . . . . . . . . . . . . . . . . . . . .13
  Academic Libraries . . . . . . . . . . . . . . . . . . . . . . . . . . . . . . . . . . . . . . . .13
  Public Libraries . . . . . . . . . . . . . . . . . . . . . . . . . . . . . . . . . . . . . . . . . . .16
  School Libraries . . . . . . . . . . . . . . . . . . . . . . . . . . . . . . . . . . . . . . . . . . .20

**BLOGGING TECHNOLOGIES SECTION** . . . . . . . . . . . . . . . . . . . . . . .23
**CHAPTER 3: Types of Blogs** . . . . . . . . . . . . . . . . . . . . . . . . . . . . . . . . .23
  Hosted Blogging Software . . . . . . . . . . . . . . . . . . . . . . . . . . . . . . . . . .23
  Server-based Blogging Software . . . . . . . . . . . . . . . . . . . . . . . . . . . . .25

**CHAPTER 4: Hosted Blogs** . . . . . . . . . . . . . . . . . . . . . . . . . . . . . . . . . . .27
  Blogger . . . . . . . . . . . . . . . . . . . . . . . . . . . . . . . . . . . . . . . . . . . . . . . . . . .28
  TypePad . . . . . . . . . . . . . . . . . . . . . . . . . . . . . . . . . . . . . . . . . . . . . . . . . .28
  LiveJournal . . . . . . . . . . . . . . . . . . . . . . . . . . . . . . . . . . . . . . . . . . . . . . .29
  WordPress.com . . . . . . . . . . . . . . . . . . . . . . . . . . . . . . . . . . . . . . . . . . .30
  Others . . . . . . . . . . . . . . . . . . . . . . . . . . . . . . . . . . . . . . . . . . . . . . . . . . . .31

**CHAPTER 5: Server-Based Blogging Solutions** . . . . . . . . . . . . . . . . . .33
  WordPress . . . . . . . . . . . . . . . . . . . . . . . . . . . . . . . . . . . . . . . . . . . . . . . .33
  Movable Type . . . . . . . . . . . . . . . . . . . . . . . . . . . . . . . . . . . . . . . . . . . . .36
  Others . . . . . . . . . . . . . . . . . . . . . . . . . . . . . . . . . . . . . . . . . . . . . . . . . . . .40

**INSTRUCTIONS/HOW TO SECTION** . . . . . . . . . . . . . . . . . . . . . . . . .43
**CHAPTER 6: Wordpress.com How To** . . . . . . . . . . . . . . . . . . . . . . . . .43
  Setting Up a Wordpress.com Weblog . . . . . . . . . . . . . . . . . . . . . . . .44
  Customizing the Look and Feel . . . . . . . . . . . . . . . . . . . . . . . . . . . . .47
  Pointers for Posting . . . . . . . . . . . . . . . . . . . . . . . . . . . . . . . . . . . . . . .48

**CHAPTER 7: Blogger How To** . . . . . . . . . . . . . . . . . . . . . . . . . . . . . . . .55
  Introduction . . . . . . . . . . . . . . . . . . . . . . . . . . . . . . . . . . . . . . . . . . . . . .55
  Setting Up a Blogger Weblog . . . . . . . . . . . . . . . . . . . . . . . . . . . . . . .56
  Customizing the Look and Feel . . . . . . . . . . . . . . . . . . . . . . . . . . . . .60
  Semi-Hosted . . . . . . . . . . . . . . . . . . . . . . . . . . . . . . . . . . . . . . . . . . . . . .63

# TABLE *of* CONTENTS *continued*

CHAPTER 8: WordPress How To . . . . . . . . . . . . . . . . . . . . . . . . . . . . . . . . . . .65

CHAPTER 9: Movable How To . . . . . . . . . . . . . . . . . . . . . . . . . . . . . . . . . . . .71
   Installing Movable Type . . . . . . . . . . . . . . . . . . . . . . . . . . . . . . . . .72
   Blogging Basics . . . . . . . . . . . . . . . . . . . . . . . . . . . . . . . . . . . . . . .79
   Customizing the Look and Feel . . . . . . . . . . . . . . . . . . . . . . . . . . . .80
   Pointers for Posting . . . . . . . . . . . . . . . . . . . . . . . . . . . . . . . . . . . .82

CHAPTER 10: Related Technologies . . . . . . . . . . . . . . . . . . . . . . . . . . . . .85
   Syndication . . . . . . . . . . . . . . . . . . . . . . . . . . . . . . . . . . . . . . . . . .85
   RSS . . . . . . . . . . . . . . . . . . . . . . . . . . . . . . . . . . . . . . . . . . . . . . .86
   Atom . . . . . . . . . . . . . . . . . . . . . . . . . . . . . . . . . . . . . . . . . . . . . .91
   Feedburner . . . . . . . . . . . . . . . . . . . . . . . . . . . . . . . . . . . . . . . . . .98
   Feed Readers . . . . . . . . . . . . . . . . . . . . . . . . . . . . . . . . . . . . . . .101
   Tagging . . . . . . . . . . . . . . . . . . . . . . . . . . . . . . . . . . . . . . . . . . .102
   Mashups . . . . . . . . . . . . . . . . . . . . . . . . . . . . . . . . . . . . . . . . . .104
   Blogging Different Types of Media . . . . . . . . . . . . . . . . . . . . . . . .106
   Photoblogging . . . . . . . . . . . . . . . . . . . . . . . . . . . . . . . . . . . . . .106
   Podcasting . . . . . . . . . . . . . . . . . . . . . . . . . . . . . . . . . . . . . . . . .107
   Videoblogging . . . . . . . . . . . . . . . . . . . . . . . . . . . . . . . . . . . . . .108
   Creative Commons . . . . . . . . . . . . . . . . . . . . . . . . . . . . . . . . . . .109

CHAPTER 11: What is Possible with a Blog? . . . . . . . . . . . . . . . . . . . . .111
   Blogs for News . . . . . . . . . . . . . . . . . . . . . . . . . . . . . . . . . . . . . .111
   Blogs for Internal Communication . . . . . . . . . . . . . . . . . . . . . . . .119
   Organizational Blogs . . . . . . . . . . . . . . . . . . . . . . . . . . . . . . . . . .121

CHAPTER 12: Blog Culture . . . . . . . . . . . . . . . . . . . . . . . . . . . . . . . . . .127
   Blog Code of Conduct . . . . . . . . . . . . . . . . . . . . . . . . . . . . . . . . .129
   Community . . . . . . . . . . . . . . . . . . . . . . . . . . . . . . . . . . . . . . . .130
   Being Native . . . . . . . . . . . . . . . . . . . . . . . . . . . . . . . . . . . . . . .131

CHAPTER 13: Future Possibilities . . . . . . . . . . . . . . . . . . . . . . . . . . . . .133

Summary . . . . . . . . . . . . . . . . . . . . . . . . . . . . . . . . . . . . . . . . . . . . . . . .145
Appendix: Blogging Tools . . . . . . . . . . . . . . . . . . . . . . . . . . . . . . . . . . .146
Glossary . . . . . . . . . . . . . . . . . . . . . . . . . . . . . . . . . . . . . . . . . . . . . . . .147
Index . . . . . . . . . . . . . . . . . . . . . . . . . . . . . . . . . . . . . . . . . . . . . . . . . . .149

# TABLE *of* FIGURES

**CHAPTER 1**

Figure 1-1    LiveJournal Home Page ................................... .4
Figure 1-2    Blogger Home Page ..................................... 5
Figure 1-3    MovableType Home Page ................................ .6
Figure 1-4    WordPress Home Page ................................... 6

**CHAPTER 2**

Figure 2-1    Ohio University Library News .......................... .14
Figure 2-2    UNC-Chapel Hill Undergraduate Library ............... .15
Figure 2-3    Virginia Tech Library News .......................... .15
Figure 2-4    WKU Libraries Blog ................................. .16
Figure 2-5    Ann Arbor District Library .......................... .17
Figure 2-6    Austin Public Library .............................. .17
Figure 2-7    Columbus Public Library Genealogy Blog ............. .18
Figure 2-8    Dover Public Library ............................... 19
Figure 2-9    Papercuts .......................................... .19
Figure 2-10   Graffiti ........................................... .20
Figure 2-11   Olson Middle School Blog ........................... .21
Figure 2-12   Rundlett Middle School Blog ........................ .21
Figure 2-13   University Laboratory High School Blog .............. .22

**CHAPTER 3**

Figure 3-1    WordPress Upgrade Screen .......................... .24
Figure 3-2    WordPress Privacy Options ......................... .24

**CHAPTER 4**

Figure 4-1    Pricing for TypePad ............................... .28
Figure 4-2    LiveJournal Home Page ............................. .29
Figure 4-3    Pricing for LiveJournal ........................... .30
Figure 4-4    Edublogs.org ...................................... .31
Figure 4-5    Class Blogmeister ................................. .32

**CHAPTER 5**

Figure 5-1    WordPress Plugins Web Page ........................ .34
Figure 5-2    WordPress Pages Screen ............................ .34
Figure 5-3    Akismet Spam Catcher ............................. .35
Figure 5-4    WordPress User Administration ..................... .36
Figure 5-5    Movable Type Plugins Screen ...................... .37
Figure 5-6    Movable Type Comments Screen ..................... .37
Figure 5-7    Movable Type User Management ..................... .38
Figure 5-8    Movable Type Asset Management Feature ............. .38
Figure 5-9    UThink Project Web Site .......................... .39
Figure 5-10   Typo Sidebar Widgets .............................. .40
Figure 5-11   Madison Jefferson County Public Library Blog ....... .41
Figure 5-12   Ann Arbor District Library Web Site ............... .42

# TABLE *of* FIGURES *continued*

**CHAPTER 6**

Figure 6-1    WordPress Account Creation Form ........................45
Figure 6-2    WordPress Blog Creation Form .........................45
Figure 6-3    WordPress Login Screen ................................46
Figure 6-4    Sample Wordpress Blog Home ...........................46
Figure 6-5    WordPress Blog Administration .........................47
Figure 6-6    WordPress Theme Selection ............................47
Figure 6-7    WordPress Sidebar Customization ......................48
Figure 6-8    WordPress WYSIWYG Editor .............................49
Figure 6-9    WordPress File Upload Step 1 .........................49
Figure 6-10   WordPress File Upload Step 2 .........................50
Figure 6-11   WordPress Image Popup Window .........................50
Figure 6-12   Individual Flickr Photo Screen ......................51
Figure 6-13   YouTube Upload Step 1 ................................52
Figure 6-14   YouTube Upload Step 2 ................................52
Figure 6-15   Odeo Audio File Screen ...............................53
Figure 6-16   WordPress Blog with Odeo Audio Added to a Post ........54

**CHAPTER 7**

Figure 7-1    Blogger Home Page .....................................56
Figure 7-2    Blogger Account Creation Screen ......................56
Figure 7-3    Blogger Blog Creation Screen .........................57
Figure 7-4    Blogger Select a Template ............................58
Figure 7-5    Blogger Blog Created Screen ..........................58
Figure 7-6    Blogger WYSIWYG Editor ...............................59
Figure 7-7    Blogger Edit Posts Screen ............................59
Figure 7-8    Blogger Settings Screen ..............................60
Figure 7-9    Blogger Add Page Elements ............................61
Figure 7-10   Blogger Arrange Page Elements ........................61
Figure 7-11   Customize Blogger Template Colors ....................62
Figure 7-12   Edit Blogger Template ................................62
Figure 7-13   Blogger Set Up External Web Server ...................63
Figure 7-14   Purchase a Domain Name via Blogger ...................64

**CHAPTER 8**

Figure 8-1    WordPress Install Page ...............................67
Figure 8-2    WordPress Successfully Installed .....................68

**CHAPTER 9**

Figure 9-1    Movable Type Installation Welcome Screen .............72
Figure 9-2    Movable Type Requirements Check ......................73
Figure 9-3    Movable Type Database Configuration ..................74
Figure 9-4    Movable Type Database Configuration OK ...............75

# TABLE *of* FIGURES *continued*

Figure 9-5    Movable Type E-mail Server Configuration ................76
Figure 9-6    Movable Type Configuration Successful ...................76
Figure 9-7    Create First Movable Type User .........................77
Figure 9-8    Create First Movable Type Blog ..........................78
Figure 9-9    Movable Type Installation Successful ......................79
Figure 9-10   Movable Type Create Entry .............................80
Figure 9-11   Movable Type Select a Style ............................81
Figure 9-12   Movable Type Republish Blog ...........................81
Figure 9-13   Movable Type Asset Management .........................82
Figure 9-14   Movable Type Add New Image ...........................82
Figure 9-15   Movable Type Upload Image .............................83
Figure 9-16   Movable Type Add Image Metadata .......................83

**CHAPTER 10**
Figure 10-1   Example of Customized Netvibes Home Page ...............86
Figure 10-2   Example RSS Feed .....................................87
Figure 10-3   Example Atom Feed .....................................92
Figure 10-4   Create New Feedburner Feed .............................98
Figure 10-5   Optimize Feedburner Feed ...............................99
Figure 10-6   Analyze Feedburner Feed Traffic ........................100
Figure 10-7   Publicize the Feedburner Feed ...........................100
Figure 10-8   Tagging at Amazon.com ................................102
Figure 10-9   Example of Tag Cloud .................................103
Figure 10-10  Flickr and Blog Mashup ...............................105
Figure 10-11  Google Reader and Blog Mashup .........................105
Figure 10-12  Planet Code4Lib Web Site .............................106
Figure 10-13  LITA Blog Podcasts ...................................107

**CHAPTER 11**
Figure 11-1   PaperCuts Topeka Shawnee Public Library Blog ............112
Figure 11-2   Madison Jefferson County Public Library Kids Buzz Blog .....113
Figure 11-3   Georgia State University Photoblog ......................114
Figure 11-4   Lansing Public Library Blog ............................114
Figure 11-5   Regina Public Library New Materials Blog ................115
Figure 11-6   Darien Library Events Blog .............................116
Figure 11-7   Homer Township Public Library Teen Events Blog ..........116
Figure 11-8   Business Blog at Ohio State University Library ............117
Figure 11-9   University of Buffalo Health Sciences Library Nursing Blog ...117
Figure 11-10  NCSU Business Information Network Blog ................118
Figure 11-11  Georgia State University Library Science News Blog ........118
Figure 11-12  George Mason TripNotes Blog ..........................119
Figure 11-13  Wake Forest University Libraries Professional
              Development Blog ....................................120
Figure 11-14  Kansas Sate University Libraries SFX Documentation Blog ....121

# TABLE *of* FIGURES *continued*

Figure 11-15  ACRLog  . . . . . . . . . . . . . . . . . . . . . . . . . . . . . . . . . . . . . . . . . . . . . .122
Figure 11-16  LITA Blog . . . . . . . . . . . . . . . . . . . . . . . . . . . . . . . . . . . . . . . . . . . . .122
Figure 11-17  PLA Blog  . . . . . . . . . . . . . . . . . . . . . . . . . . . . . . . . . . . . . . . . . . . .123
Figure 11-18  Michigan Library Consortium Blog  . . . . . . . . . . . . . . . . . . . . . .123
Figure 11-19  Wisconsin Library Association Blog  . . . . . . . . . . . . . . . . . . . . . .124
Figure 11-20  Boston Regional Library System's Blog  . . . . . . . . . . . . . . . . . .125

**CHAPTER 13**
Figure 13-1   Hennepin County Library MySpace . . . . . . . . . . . . . . . . . . . . . .134
Figure 13-2   University of Texas Austin Undergraduate Library's MySpace . .135
Figure 13-3   University of Wisconsin at Madison Library's Facebook  . . . . .136
Figure 13-4   Photos on University of Wisconsin at Madison Library's
              Facebook . . . . . . . . . . . . . . . . . . . . . . . . . . . . . . . . . . . . . . . . . . . .137
Figure 13-5   Ottawa Public Library's Facebook  . . . . . . . . . . . . . . . . . . . . . .137
Figure 13-6   Scriblio at Plymouth State University  . . . . . . . . . . . . . . . . . . . .139
Figure 13-7   Scriblio RSS Feed . . . . . . . . . . . . . . . . . . . . . . . . . . . . . . . . . . . .139
Figure 13-8   Cook Memorial Public Library . . . . . . . . . . . . . . . . . . . . . . . . . .140
Figure 13-9   WordPress Reading Options  . . . . . . . . . . . . . . . . . . . . . . . . . . .141
Figure 13-10  Beyond Brown Paper  . . . . . . . . . . . . . . . . . . . . . . . . . . . . . . . . .142
Figure 13-11  Commented Digital Object at Beyond Brown Paper  . . . . . . . .142
Figure 13-12  Western Springs History  . . . . . . . . . . . . . . . . . . . . . . . . . . . . . . 143
Figure 13-13  Example Comment from Great Lakes Images Web Site  . . . . . . .143
Figure 13-14  Combined Arms Research Library Flickr Photoblog . . . . . . . . . .144
Figure 13-15  Redwood City History Flickr Photoblog  . . . . . . . . . . . . . . . . . .144

# ABOUT *the* AUTHORS

## KAREN A. COOMBS

Karen A. Coombs serves as the Head of Web Services at the University of Houston Libraries. Her duties include development and maintenance of the libraries' Web site and electronic presence. She has an MLS and an MS in Information Management from Syracuse University. Karen has presented at many national conferences including ALA Annual, LITA Forum, and Internet Librarian; she has written articles for *Computers in Libraries, Library Journal, Library Hi Tech,* and *Journal of Academic Librarianship.* She is co-chair of the LITA special interest group for Blogs, Wikis and Other New Interactive Media (BIGWIG), a member of the LITA Top Technology Trends panel, and the author of the Library Web Chic weblog <http://librarywebchic.net>.

*Photo by Dawn Van Hall*

## JASON GRIFFEY

Jason is currently an Assistant Professor and Head of Library Information Technology at the University of Tennessee at Chattanooga. He received his MLS from the University of North Carolina at Chapel Hill, and did graduate work in philosophy at Ohio University. His research interests include technology in higher education, copyright law, and social software. His blog, Pattern Recognition, can be found at <http://www.jasongriffey.net/wp> and has been active since 2003. He has written for *Library Journal*; presented at Computers in Libraries, ALA Annual, Five Weeks to a Social Library, and other national and international conferences; and has been featured on BoingBoing and Digg.

*Photo by Iris Jastram*

He lives in Sewanee, Tennessee, with his wife Dr. Betsy Sandlin and their daughter Eliza. In his spare time, he plays games, reads obsessively, and plans for the inevitable zombie uprising.

# INTRODUCTION

How do two people who have never worked in the same library and live more than 800 miles apart, come together to write a book on blogging in libraries? In January of 2006 we—Jason Griffey and Karen Coombs—began working together as part of the Library and Information Technology Association's (LITA) special interest group on Blogs, Wikis and Other New Interactive Media (BIGWIG). Both of us had professional blogs, and we wanted to see LITA's blog become a successful communication tool for the organization and to promote the use of blogs in libraries. To further this end, BIGWIG developed a program for the 2006 American Library Association's Annual Conference. The program focused on blogs in libraries. It provided a mix of technical how-to, why libraries should create blogs, and best practices for a successful blog. The program was a resounding success, with a room so packed that there wasn't even space to sit on the floor. Afterwards, because we were featured speakers as part of the program, we were approached to write a book about blogging in libraries. At first, we were hesitant; other books on blogging in libraries were in progress. However, we eventually decided the kind of book about blogging in libraries that we wanted to write wasn't published or being written.

We set out to write a book that would be useful to librarians and libraries blogging on multiple knowledge levels, from techie librarians to administrators to reference librarians. The purpose of the book is to provide librarians and libraries with information crucial to developing and maintaining effective blogs. There are several pieces to this puzzle: from basic information about weblogs and how they can be used to technical information about how to set up and maintain a weblog. In this book we try to give readers the tools not only to start their own library weblog but also to explore the multitude of potential ways in which blogs can be used in libraries. To do all this we've put together a book that is both an overview of the landscape of blogging in libraries and provides technical how-to and guidebook information.

We wanted to create a book that combined both technical and non-technical information about blogs. The first chapter, "An Introduction to Blogs," focuses on how blogs originated on the Web and discuss the characteristics of a blog. Chapter 2 extends upon this idea and discusses why a library might want to create a blog and how blogs can be used in a variety of library settings from the school library to the special library. Chapters 3, 4, and 5 are part of the "Blogging Technologies Section." This section of the book discusses different types of tools that can be used for creating blogs, the differences between them, and the pros and cons of the different types of tools.

The next section of the book, "How To," is also technical in nature. In this section we discuss how to get setup and how to blog using a variety of blogging tools. Chapters 6 and 7 provide how-to information for two different hosted blogging tools: WordPress.com and Blogger. Chapters 8 and 9 discuss server-based blogging tools: WordPress and Movable Type.

There are many other technologies and tools of which bloggers should be aware. Chapter 10 focuses on these "Related Technologies." This chapter includes a discussion of syndication, tagging, and Creative Commons. In Chapter 11, "What is Possible with a Blog?," readers learn about how blogs are being used in libraries. Chapter 12 discusses Blog Culture, issues of ethics in blogging, and social conventions. In the final chapter we speculate on where blogs are going and what "blogging" might look like in the future.

Although this book can be read from cover to cover, many readers may already know something about blogs and the technology behind them. As a result, the book is divided into chapters and sections that focus on a particular topic. For example, if you are interesting in learning how to set up and run a Movable Type weblog, then Chapter 9 is for you. By the same token, not all topics related to blogs are technical ones. Therefore, there are also chapters that focus on how a library might choose to use a blog. If you need to make a decision about which blogging software might be best for your institution, then make sure you read the "Blogging Technologies Section".

We learned many new things about blogs writing the book. Some of these things surprised us because we thought we knew particular technologies really well! As a result, although you may not read this book from cover to cover initially, we suggest that you think about reading all the sections at some point. Consequently, you will probably learn something new about blogs in libraries!

# CHAPTER 1

# An Introduction
# to Blogs

## What is a Blog?

No single definition of the word "blog" will suffice to be completely descriptive of either the form or function of this specific type of online publication. A blog is a type of Web site, but that's a bit like describing the New York Times as a type of newspaper...often, the sum of the parts is more than expected. It's a bit like attempting to define the things that make up a book. What is a book? How hard would it be to come up with a definitive description of all of the things in the world that we call "book?" Books come in all shapes and sizes, can contain near-infinite types of information in thousands of different languages, and can be made of nearly any material. We expect, when we hear the word, that the object will have pages made of pulped vegetable matter, and will consist of words placed in a sequence that allows someone, somewhere to decode their meanings. However it is easily imagined that we might come across an object that had none of these properties, and we might still call it a book.

Thus is the nature of definitions. Trying to define "blog" isn't any easier. So you may need to bear with us for a bit before we get to the answer.

Blog is short for weblog, which is descriptive of the early purpose of these sites, but again it misses the forest for the trees. So let's begin simply, by looking at the pieces that came together in the very early part of the 21st century to produce this branch in the evolution of information distribution. The early World Wide Web was based around flat HTML files, text files with metadata associated with certain parts of the page that told the browser how the page should look and whether there were links, pictures, or other objects embedded in the text. In the late 90s and very early 21st century, there was a move towards more complicated, but more elegant, methods of Web site maintenance. This began with the separation of content and style via Cascading Style Sheets (CSS) where the HTML contains just the content and the CSS applied to the content tells the browser how the content should be presented. This allows for a level of abstraction of the content that becomes very powerful when applied to larger Web sites since you can now alter the look and feel of the entire site with the editing of one file, rather than needing to be concerned with each and every piece of content.

The next step in the development of content abstraction was that of the database-driven Web site. This was driven by more and more powerful and easy-to-use programming languages on the Web, primarily Perl and PHP, and the availability of cheap or free databases software like MySQL and PostGRE. This allows content to be stored and retrieved from a database and makes the content itself modular. A "page" is just a line of programming language that calls content from a database, and then CSS tells it what it should look like. The whole thing ends up in HTML, but that's almost an afterthought of the browser, the "window" into the dynamic world of the new net, Web 2.0. The browser "speaks" HTML, but the underpinnings of the actual document you see are increasingly other languages, and the content is stored in a metadata rich format inside a database waiting to be called into duty.

About now you're probably asking yourself what this has to do with blogs. It has everything to do with them, at least everything to do with their rise into the public consciousness. When updating a Web site meant either opening the HTML and hand-coding the desired look or the use of a middle-ware product like Dreamweaver® that did most of the heavy-lifting coding for you, most people couldn't be bothered to update their pages daily. Some of course will, and those early pioneers showed the wider Web the problem. Blogger, LiveJournal, Movable Type, and others solved this difficulty by involving these processes of metadata, databases, and programming languages in the background.

It sounds, at least initially, as if this is a more complex way to do things. How can increasing the number of tools used make for a simpler solution? The brilliance comes from the fact that the user doesn't have to know, care, or see any of those complexities. The increased flexibility of the tools allowed a simple, straightforward interface to feed these databases full of content. The style, look, and feel of the site could be pre-loaded by these new web services, leaving it to the end-user to do nothing but provide content...which, as it turns out, people are very willing to do. That is what Blogger and LiveJournal did: they took 99 percent of the effort of getting started with a blog out of the equation. Then Movable Type burst onto the scene by offering the most fully featured software for the more IT advanced of the early adopters. While initial setup of Movable Type did take some skill, the daily updating was literally push-button in its simplicity. It is this simplicity of updating that truly makes the format of the blog possible.

And we come to the first part of our definition: a blog is (usually) a Web page written in a programming language where the content of the site is stored in a meta-data-rich format. The problem with this part of the definition is that 99 percent of the people who read blogs have no idea this is the case. The language and content storage are completely invisible to the consumer, so how does someone who just reads the Web know when something is a blog and when something isn't?

Blogs tend to follow a specific format, at least to the degree where it is possible to recognize them simply by form. The format of the blog is different depending on the exact purpose and nature of the information being presented, although there are some accepted standards. The most widely embraced aspect of a blog is its organization. Since one of the hallmarks of the form is frequent updates, there needs to be some way to determine the new content from the old. The easiest possible method of this is the standard: organization of the page in reverse chronological order, with new information at the top descending into the old as you scroll down. This is the most commonly cited method of determining a Web page is a blog.

There are other typical hallmarks of a blog. One of these is that the individual posts are the result of a single author, usually named (even if the posts are anonymous, there is generally a *nom de plume* associated with posts). Blogs are regularly updated, although regular can sometimes mean daily, weekly, or even less frequently. Some have multiple posts a day. Some are just lists of links. Some are simply photos with no text associated with them, while the posts of still other blogs are audio files.

We can now add to our building definition of blog: a blog is a Web page (usually) written in a programming language where the content of the site is stored in a metadata-rich format, and the presentation of the content is (usually) in a reverse chronological format. Each piece of content is (usually) the product of a single author, and the content is updated regularly.

There is another technical piece that we must introduce in order to understand what a blog is. Since blogs are composed of regularly updated content, they are ideal candidates for syndication. Each post can be delivered as an individual piece while still being linked back to the larger whole of the blog. The format that syndicates blog posts is called RSS, Rich Site Syndication or Really Simple Syndication depending on where you get your definition of the initialism. RSS will be discussed in a later chapter more fully. However, it is one of the key parts of a successful blog.

A large percentage of blogs allows for comments on posts, and comments are one of two things that add a social aspect to blogs. Comments are the feature of blogs that allow readers to give feedback on any given entry. The permission for submitting comments can be set at nearly any level. Some bloggers allow for anyone to comment on their work, even with complete anonymity. Others insist on having a name/e-mail attached to a comment, even if that name/e-mail is invented. Still others exclusively allow for registered users to comment, ensuring that only people who are a part of the existing community can comment. Other bloggers do not allow comments at all, preferring their work to be the focus of the site. Comments are certainly not necessary for the form, but more blogs allow comments than don't.

Movable Type introduced a technology known as "trackback" in early versions of its software, which is the other piece of the social puzzle for blogs. Trackback was a simple idea that became powerful in execution. It was, essentially, a method of knowing who was talking about your blog online. If Person A posted on his blog and referenced an entry of Person B, Person B would get a trackback notice to let her know that Person A had mentioned her. This allowed for an increased capacity to follow the discussion of your ideas online and added greatly to the social connectivity of blogs.

The final working definition for the purposes of this book, then, is that a blog is a Web page (usually) written in a programming language where the content of the site is stored in a metadata-rich format, and the presentation of the content is (usually) in a reverse chronological format. Each piece of content is (usually) the product of a single author, and the content is updated regularly. The page in question (usually) has some form of social component, whether through comments, trackback, or other mechanism of communicating content or feedback.

# History of Blogging

The timeline for the rise of the blog on the Internet is fuzzy, but there are some clear watershed moments that led to the rise of the form. The two sites that kicked off the common use of the blog were LiveJournal and Blogger, which both launched in 1999, with LiveJournal predating Blogger by five months. Prior to these sites, several individuals had been creating online logs or diaries of their daily activity manually by simply updating the HTML pages for each new entry. These sites led the way by outlining the form that blogs would use while clever programmers worked out the automation of the code creation using the PHP/Perl/MySQL solutions. So while blogging predates the tools we now associate with it, it did not really come into its own until the tools were available and the barrier to entry was low enough that setting up and maintaining a blog was a trivial process.

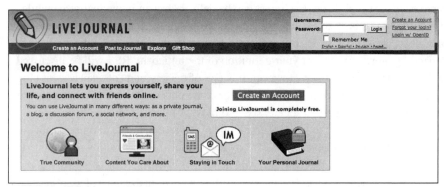

**Figure 1-1:** LiveJournal Home Page

LiveJournal is a community of blogs, each associated with a LiveJournal member. The aspect of LiveJournal that set it apart from Blogger is that it is a closed community. There is no open signup, and in order to become a member of the community you have to be invited by an already existing member. This led LiveJournal to become a very popular destination for teens, because there was a built in exclusionary feel to it—only your friends were there, more or less. LiveJournal is still a popular blogging service for teens, but it isn't typically used by libraries or professionals due to the exclusive nature of the community.

Blogger, on the other hand, made blogging a possibility for the average Internet user. It required no setup other than signing up, similar to the sort of signup for a Web-based e-mail account (Hotmail®, Gmail™, etc.), and you had a blog of your very own, updated through a friendly interface. Blogger provided the storage for your blog, maintained upgrades, and added features over time. It is difficult to imagine an easier way to set up a blog than this. This is why Blogger found itself in 2003 being purchased by Google, who still owns the service and has upgraded the reliability and features several times since acquiring it. The rise in popularity of blogging is linked with the ease of use of Blogger

**Figure 1-2:** Blogger Home Page

Two other pieces of software led the more technical charge into blogging: Movable Type and WordPress. Both are more complicated to set up, requiring server-based installation on the part of the user. WordPress came onto the scene much later than the other blogging solutions, not hitting the Web until 2003. Until that point, Movable Type was the clear leader for technically inclined bloggers who wanted more direct control over their software and were not happy with a hosted solution. Movable Type is, however, proprietary software, while WordPress is an open source product. Movable Type allowed for free use of the software to individuals, but WordPress is free to all types of users. It is difficult to compete with free, especially when the free solution is robustly supported online. Over the course of the last four years, there has been a reversal in the popularity of Movable Type and WordPress, with WordPress currently being, from all appearances, the most popular installed blogging solution.

**Figure 1-3:** Movable Type Home Page

**Figure 1-4:** WordPress Home Page

As far as libraries, librarians were early adopters of blogs. Several prominent librarians began blogging very early, even before there was software to take the work out of the updating. To some degree, dated lists of favorite Web sites, a very common form of an early library Web site, is a form of a blog. Jenny Levine created one of the earliest of these with her site The Librarians' Site du Jour, which ran from 1995 until 1999. She then turned it into a more "blog-like" blog, rechristened it The Shifted Librarian in 2002, and it has been running continuously since. Librarian Steven Cohen is another of the early adopters who blog about libraries, having started his blog LibraryStuff in August 2000. The first official ALA blog was launched by the Public Library Association in 2005, but there are dozens of ALA blogs at the time of this writing, ranging from the Library Information Technology Association Blog to the ALA TechSource blog.

# Why Blog?

Blogging can fill many roles in the typical library and several roles specific to the many different types of libraries. Many people blog simply because they have something to say, to air their point of view, or to comment on things they feel strongly about. When you get down to the basic nature of a blog, it's just the regular temporal presentation of information or material, and libraries are certainly about the presentation of information.

Consider carefully why to start a blog by asking what purpose the blog will serve in your particular situation. What information are you trying to share? New events at the library, new books, updates on classes offered? Do you need an internal reporting mechanism for common reference questions? Any of these regularly changing sets of information could be handled by a blog. In addition to being a good gathering mechanism for a variety of different kinds of information, there are significant advantages to using blogging software to manage information presentation.

The first good reason to use a blog over another method of information presentation is that blogging software acts as a sort of miniature content management system. The use of templates and a database for the content simplifies the creation of content to the point where you don't have to worry about the look and feel of the page. You can concentrate on making the content as good as it can possibly be and not worry about the way it will look, because the blog is going to present it just as the template looks.

The second huge advantage for blogs is that because of the structure and the way they store content in a metadata-rich format there is a far greater ability to find a blog rather than a traditional Web site. Each post on a blog typically has its own permanent URL that can be referred back to. Also, since temporal organization is a cornerstone of blogs, finding posts from specific days/dates is very easy. As well, most blogging software provides different levels of metadata for application to individual posts, like categories or tags, which allow for additional levels of search.

The third reason for using blogs in libraries has to do with the social aspects of the form. Since most blogs have some component that allows for feedback, whether by direct comment or trackback from another blog, there is a sort of conversation that develops after a blog is around for a bit. The ability for patrons to potentially comment on discussions about the library is a powerful tool, if libraries will listen. If libraries and librarians truly want to focus on the patron and work towards a patron-centered library, blogs are one mechanism for gathering feedback from patrons.

Much like any form of content creation, the actual question shouldn't be, "Why blog?" but instead, "What information need is there that a blog can fill?" Blogs can make information distribution easier, and the key is to figure out how a blog can help your staff or patrons access your information more easily (or conversely, make it easier for librarians to provide information). In many cases there is some simple communication that would be well served by a blog. An internal blog that alerts the faculty and staff to facility issues in the library, a new book blog that updates faculty or students on the new books in the library, or a tool for outreach to the community to share the cool new stuff that you're doing are all appropriate sorts of information that fit well into a blog format.

The format is the key. Any information that is time-limited or sensitive and lends itself to short, news-like posts is a good candidate for a blog.

The thing that sets blogs apart from other technologies as a Web presence is that nearly all blog software automatically provides for RSS feeds of its content. Rich Site Syndication allows for an enormous amount of re-use of the content in question. You can embed it into another site, combine it with other feeds using a service like Feedburner™ or Yahoo! Pipes, have users subscribe to it using an aggregator, have it e-mailed somewhere using a service like RSSFWD, or any number of other things. It makes the content flexible in ways that static creation simply can't compete with. In later chapters we will discuss many methods of using RSS to provide information in ways outside of the standard blog format.

## *Sociology of Blogging*

Earlier in the chapter we briefly discussed some of the social aspects of blogs, things like trackback and comments. Very early in the development of blogs, a norm solidified around something that came to be called a blogroll. A blogroll is a list on a static area of your blog (usually a sidebar) where you name other blogs you read or Web sites that interest you. In the very early days of the blogosphere—the universe of blogs on the Internet—it was considered polite to link to someone who linked to you, reciprocating the advantage that linking gives in search engine results. This isn't the case as much these days, but it was an important social dynamic early in the formation of blogs. As you increased the number of links coming into your blog, it went up in Google™ search results and more and more reader traffic was driven to it. If you were linked by a particularly popular blog, your readership could skyrocket overnight. There are several names for this occurrence online, the earliest of which is the Slashdot Effect, named after the popular "News for Nerds" blog and often shortened to "being slash-dotted."

From this web of links, you can form a type of reputation economy. Indeed, that's exactly how Google gives us such good results for searches, by analyzing the frequency of the terms as they relate to Web site reputation in the form of links. People began to parse these reputations manually, hopping from one blog to the other by following the blogrolls. Navigating these early communities in the blogosphere, where you would find a tightly interconnected set of blogs (with a few outliers) was like jumping from stone to stone in a pond.

From the emergent reputation economy, it was reasonably easy to identify connectors and see who was influential within a given group of blogs. By looking at the time of post and seeing how the information propagated from one blog to the other like ripples in a pond, you could see who was creating useful information and who was passing it on. You also could begin to see a structure of the distribution of news and information. When you combine the web of links and this propagation information, you can identify the blogs that are central to the information economy. These blogs are generally given a higher level of trust and are certainly given a higher level of attention and readership. This process is analogous to the reputation of academic journals but on a much shorter timeline. Journals gain trust and reputation through peer review and citation ranking, which are very closely related to the mechanisms described above only on a timeline of years or decades instead of, in the case of blogs, weeks or months.

Because of the speed with which reputation is built via blogs, it doesn't take long for a "top tier" of blogs and bloggers to emerge. One thing that is different in this online reputation economy, as compared to academic journals, is that it is often the personality of the blogger in question, the "voice," that leads to one blog standing out among the cacophony of other voices. The information conveyed is still central to popularity, but the voice of the blogger has a great deal to do with a given blog's popularity. Some of the early blogs and bloggers that stood above the fold include Jason Kottke and the group blog BoingBoing (subtitle: A Directory of Wonderful Things).

With trackbacks and comments, a dialogue can be created from blog to blog. When someone creates a post that references one of your posts, it will show up in the comments section of your blog letting you know that someone has referenced your content. You can then follow it, comment on his post, or post something referencing his blog, all of which is shown to the reader in the form of links. This built-in conversational technology, when combined with the reputation economy, really pushed the platform of blogs into a new staple of the Web 2.0 informational environment.

Blogs allow for the sharing of information, conversation regarding the information, automatic archival with metadata attached, and the reuse of the information in an uncountable number of ways...why wouldn't librarians be entranced with them?

# CHAPTER 2

# *Why a Library Blog?*

Why would your library want a blog? Does your library need a blog? These two questions have been the core of many meetings at libraries over the last couple of years. There are many things blogs do well. All too often those not familiar with the form start at the wrong end of the blog equation, and the end result is the same as any poorly thought-out execution of technology. The blog format lends itself to information that has certain characteristics: regularly updated, single authorship, temporally focused. News items, as an example, are a perfect sort of information to use within a blog...they are generally tied to a specific time period and are regularly updated. New books would be a library-specific example of an excellent use of the blog form.

There are many things for which people think to use blogs that are not always the best use of the technology. Blogs are not the right answer for static content (at least not a blog *qua* blog) or for information that regularly changes or needs updating. There are ways to utilize some blog software to do those things, but neither is native to the form. Blogs are not the right answer for pages of policies or for highly structured information (spreadsheets, etc). Some blog software (here making the distinction between the form and the code) will manage these sorts of information for you, but this use doesn't typify the medium.

Generally, what is it about the blog form that is useful for every library type? There are a few reasons that stand out: to act as a portal for news for patrons, to accommodate internal communication, or to serve as a technological tool where you are leveraging the technology behind the blog for a specific end.

## Blog as News Portal

By far the most common use of a blog is as a news portal for patrons. Whether you are keeping patrons updated with workshop and instructional opportunities, letting them know about special events in the library, or just announcing new books, the blog is the perfect method. The temporal organization and the automatic archival allows for easy browsing of new and old information. If the blog is regularly updated, it's a place that patrons can come to and expect to find the newest information from your library.

There are many advantages to using the blog form for news items. One is that the blog allows the person writing the entry to nearly forget about form and concentrate only on content. The software handles the form and layout, and the person updating the blog can be at any level of computer comfort. No HTML coding is necessary, just write the entry and press a button. This allows the news to be updated by the person directly rather than being passed to a "Web person" before the update can happen. Democratization of news creation is a huge benefit to using a blog platform.

For internal communication, a blog is a great method of keeping people updated without abusing e-mail. Especially in large libraries, there may be things that everyone needs to know: a database is acting up, there's a water leak on the third floor, or the library has purchased a new resource. If staff are separated by distance, a blog is a great way to share with everyone without the need of sending 40 different e-mails. The blog timeline again helps with this, since staff can always see what the newest piece of information is by just hitting reload. Using the categories available in most blog software allows you to establish the blog as a knowledge base as well. Need to know how many times someone reported a problem on the third floor? Just click on the category on the blog, and you can see all of the times that someone has reported a problem and what those problems were. This is very useful for management within the library.

It is also possible to use blog software purely for the technological side-effect: an easily updated RSS feed. Some libraries have used a blog purely as a method of producing repurposable content pieces for other parts of their Web presence. As an example, you could have a "new book" section of your Web site that simply pulled the RSS feed from a blog that wasn't publicized as a destination (or could even suppress the HTML completely). The Web site would act as the display for the information without the traditional chronological page to visit. The advantage of a blog for this purpose is that the posting interface is usually very easy to use, much easier than a traditional HTML editor. This would make it possible for librarians and staff who feel uncomfortable creating content for the Web to use this easy interface to provide content.

# Internal Communication

Blogs are an excellent method of reducing e-mail updates to staff about internal issues. While most blogs are publicly available on the Web, it is possible to limit the access to a blog in different ways. Several Web-based blogging services such as Blogger allow the blog owner to easily set permission for access to the blog. However, limiting access to a blog that runs on server-based blogging software require some familiarity with the Web server that you use and access to the server itself, so it may take some assistance from your IT staff to make a private blog work. Depending on what you choose to share via the blog, you may not need to make it private at all.

There are advantages to using a blog for basic internal communication things, the ability to categorize for later retrieval, create a single source for staff to check for updates, and repurpose the information via RSS if needed. For an internal blog dedicated to keeping staff updated, you may have a series of basic categories that the updates fall under, for example, building issues, circulation, IT issues, and personnel. Since blog software keeps track of which posts are in which category, it is very easy to see that you've had eight IT issues this month. This categorization of problems isn't possible with email reporting, since email is a distributed communication method while a blog is a centralized communication point. Centralization also means that all staff can stay current with what's happening in the library without having to send 20 different e-mails or rely on department heads or section leaders to send out updates. Using a blog for internal communication also means that you get all of the benefits of RSS that we'll discuss later in the book including the ability to automatically send the information where you want it. If you decide to push the news to other parts of campus but don't want another department to have access to the actual blog, RSS allows that. Or say that you just want to be able to send the IT news to the campus IT department, RSS allows that flexibility. If people still want to get the information by e-mail, even that is possible by setting up an RSS system. The levels of flexibility inherent in the blog platform makes it a great option for internal communications.

# Academic Libraries

Academic libraries have found many different ways to leverage blogging software, some of them having little to do with the actual blog form and more to do with the functionality of the software in converting information to RSS. Within the scope of the academic libraries position on campus, there are many roles for blogs: internal communication, external marketing, instruction, as a reference tool, and a place to highlight new and interesting resources. Here are a few examples of academic libraries and their blogs, annotated with discussion of why this is a good use for a blog.

*Ohio University Library News*
<http://www.library.ohiou.edu/newsblog>

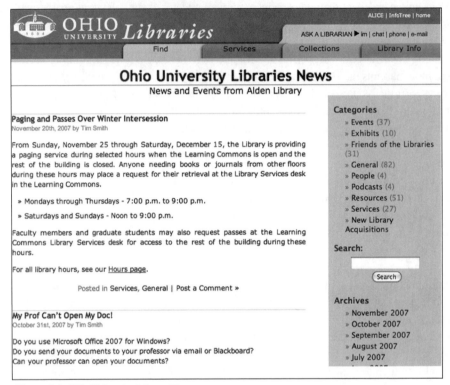

**Figure 2-1:** Ohio University Library News

A very active blog, dating from very early in the birth of the library blog (2003), this blog is used by Ohio University to post general library announcements and notices of new information sources. Things that make this an outstanding academic library blog include the use of categories that allow users to select specific areas of interest, the extensive archives that let people browse the timeline easily, and the integration of the header from the library home page giving the user a uniform user experience.

## University of North Carolina at Chapel Hill RB House Undergraduate Library
<http://www.lib.unc.edu/house/ul_blog.html>

**Figure 2-2:** UNC-Chapel Hill Undergraduate Library

UNC-Chapel Hill uses this blog as a platform to announce new resources, but it deals primarily with database resources. It includes useful summaries of the database coverage and specific contents.

## Virginia Tech Library News
<http://news.lib.vt.edu/libnews/index.php>

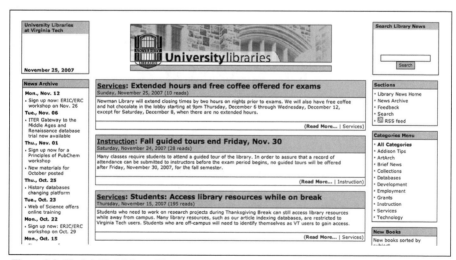

**Figure 2-3:** Virginia Tech Library News

This is another good example of an academic library using a blog to push news, including instructional opportunities for students. This blog is integrated into the larger library Web site in a way that other examples haven't been, using a content management system called PHP-Nuke to handle both the blog and the larger Web presence of the library.

## Western Kentucky University Libraries Blog
<http:// blog.wku.edu/library/>

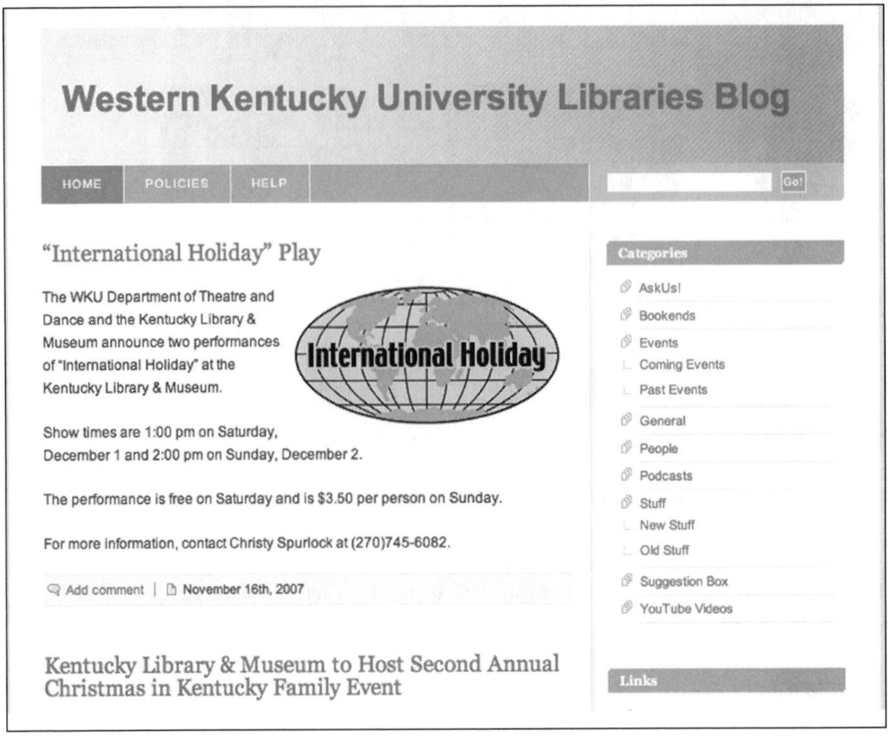

**Figure 2-4:** WKU Libraries Blog

A beautiful example of a WordPress blog, this library blog at WKU has upcoming events, workshop information, and community/university events all gathered together in an attractive, easy-to-navigate package.

# Public Libraries

Public libraries are using blogs primarily as another form of online marketing to reach out to their community and involve them in the activities of the library. The blog form is nearly unparalleled as a news medium, and the public library blogs have become a central part of getting the word out about new books, programs, and events.

Here are just a few of the exemplary public library blogs:

### Ann Arbor District Library
<http://www.aadl.org/>

**Figure 2-5:** Ann Arbor District Library

The Ann Arbor District Library has long been on the cutting edge of library technology, so it probably shouldn't be a surprise that their home page is their blog. This makes sure that the newest information is always front-and-center when patrons visit its site. It also makes it easy for patrons to subscribe via RSS if they want, and the AADL has made sure that patrons can get information at multiple levels of granularity by classifying its blog posts no less than 92 different ways with RSS feed for each of them <http://www.aadl.org/syndication>.

### Austin Public Library
<http://www.austinpubliclibraryblog.blogspot.com/>

**Figure 2-6:** Austin Public Library

Austin is using a hosted blogging solution for its blog, in this case, Blogger. This blog is linked from its library home page <http://www.ci.austin.tx.us/library/> and is used as a method of highlighting aspects of their collection on an ongoing basis. As an example, see the September 12, 2007, post on Johnny Cash <http://austinpubliclibraryblog.blogspot.com/2007/09/man-in-black.html>, which highlights the anniversary of his death and the materials available at the Austin Public Library that involve the Man in Black.

### Columbus Public Library Genealogy and Local History Section
<http://www.columbuspublic-genealogy.blogspot.com/>

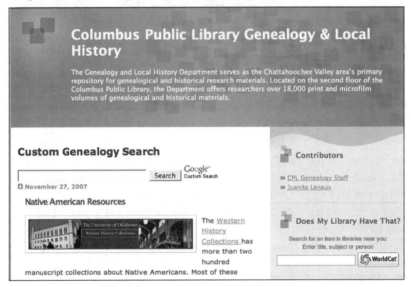

**Figure 2-7:** Columbus Public Library Genealogy Blog

In some cases, a subsection of a library, instead of the library as a whole, may have a blog presence. Such is the case at the Columbus (OH) Public Library, where the genealogy section has a blog that outlines new tools and strategies for genealogical research in Ohio. Also a hosted blog (Blogger), this example demonstrates how much detail you can customize even with a hosted solution. The library has embedded videos in the sidebar, a Worldcat search, and an amazing blogroll: a full-featured example for others to follow.

### Dover Public Library
<http://doverpl.blogspot.com/>

The Dover Public Library blog is a perfect example of simple, straightforward application of the blog to meet library needs. The blog is used as a marketing tool, updating people on happenings and promoting things like Banned Books Week and other events at the library. In addition, the library is using Blogger (you can tell by the .blogspot.com URL), which means it does not have to worry about hosting, upkeep, backup, or anything else. Librarians can just blog and let Google take care of the rest. This is a simple solution for public libraries without the IT department that most academic libraries would have.

**Figure 2-8:** Dover Public Library

## *Topeka and Shawnee County Public Library*
<http://www.tscpl.org/papercuts>

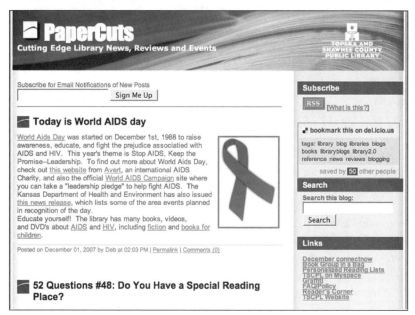

**Figure 2-9:** Papercuts

The Topeka and Shawnee County Public Library has not one but two blogs. Papercuts is the adult-oriented blog for news, new books, and library news. Graffiti is the equivalent for teens/young adults. Both use Moveable Type as a server-based blog solution. The other best-practice to pull from these is that both have the RSS feed which is easily available for the blog, and listed at the top of the sidebar with both the classic RSS orange image and a supplementary page that allows for subscription to a number of their feeds at once. That is a great feature for readers who have discovered the power of an RSS aggregator/feed reader.

<http://www.tscpl.org/graffiti>

**Figure 2-10:** Graffiti

# School Libraries

School libraries have used the blog to reach out, as public libraries do, but they are often focused on presenting specific resources to the students—and parents—of their school. School library blogs are often used as a 21st century bulletin board, a place to post announcements and things of importance to the students they serve. Blogs in a school library environment allow for conversation between parents, children, and administrators to develop and flourish in ways that are very difficult to manage outside the format. The advantages of blogs in this conversation is that they are public and technologies like trackback allow the conversation to range from blog to blog and still easily be followed. The disadvantage of blogs for school libraries is the same: they are public, and because school library patrons are almost exclusively minors, there are laws in the United States about the amount of information that can be transmitted about them.

School libraries often use blogs in a manner similar to academic libraries, to push information about new books out into the world and to present timely notice of databases or other digital resources that can be used for research.

Here are a couple of great examples of school libraries using blogs to reach out to students:

### Olson Middle School
<http://omsbookblog.blogspot.com/>

Olson Middle School in Bloomington, Minnesota, is using its blog to review books for students and parents alike. The best thing about this blog is the categories that the books are placed in: A Guy Book, both Futuristic Fiction and Science Fiction, Girl Problems, and Dogs. These labels are far more telling for the middle school audience than the Library of Congress subject headings would be.

**Figure 2-11:** Olson Middle School Blog

### Rundlett Middle School
<http://blueduke.blogspot.com/>

Rundlett Middle is in Concord, New Hampshire and is using its blog as a book review area for students. This blog has been around for a very long time in the library blog world, since 2004, and is a great look at current reading trends as well as historical ones. Never underestimate the value of historical data like this, especially when it comes time to do collection development or justify budgetary items.

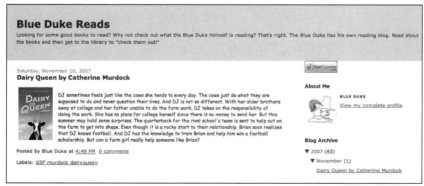

**Figure 2-12:** Rundlett Middle School Blog

*University Laboratory High School Library*
<http://www.uni.uiuc.edu/library/blog/>

**Figure 2-13:** University Laboratory High School Blog

This blog from University Laboratory High School in Urbana, Illinois, departs from the book review format and instead becomes a general information site where the librarian has a place to talk. It is much more traditional blog format and a great example of open dialogue with your students.

One interesting note is that many school library blogs use Blogger as their platform. This is understandable, since school libraries very rarely have access to a server that would enable WordPress or other options. ULHS does have Blogger uploading to a server, which is a great example of a hybrid approach that other school libraries could potentially mimic.

# BLOGGING TECHNOLOGIES SECTION

CHAPTER 3

# *Types of Blogs*

In terms of technology there are basically two types of blogging solutions: hosted blogging software and server-based blogging software. Hosted blogging software is a solution where the blogging software is operated by the developer, requiring no software installation for the weblog author. Server-based blogging software is a solution that is installed by weblog authors to run on their own systems. Each type of blogging software has its own advantages and disadvantages.

## *Hosted Blogging Software*

Hosted blogging software is operated and maintained by a developer company that takes responsibility for the maintenance of the software. There are several different hosted solutions for blogging currently available. Some of the most popular include LiveJournal, TypePad, WordPress.com, and Blogger. Additionally, some social networking applications such as MySpace offer blogging as part of their suite of service. Most of these solutions offer basic services free but charge an additional fee for more extensive services. For example, a custom CSS or an unlimited number of users on a blog can cost extra.

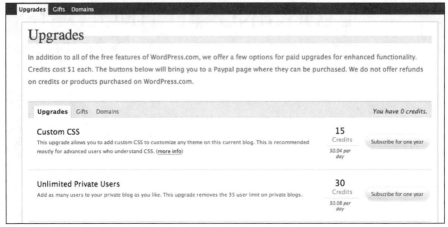

**Figure 3-1:** WordPress Upgrade Screen

Some of the hosted solutions allow you to have many blogs with many authors. This is the case with both Blogger and WordPress.com where a blog can have multiple authors and a single account can have many blogs. However, with both of these systems blog owners have to make sure that all the authors they want to be able to post to their blogs are members of the service. Another feature some hosted-solutions offer is the ability to make your blog private. Both Blogger and WordPress.com allow you to create a blog that is password-protected and only available to users whom you choose.

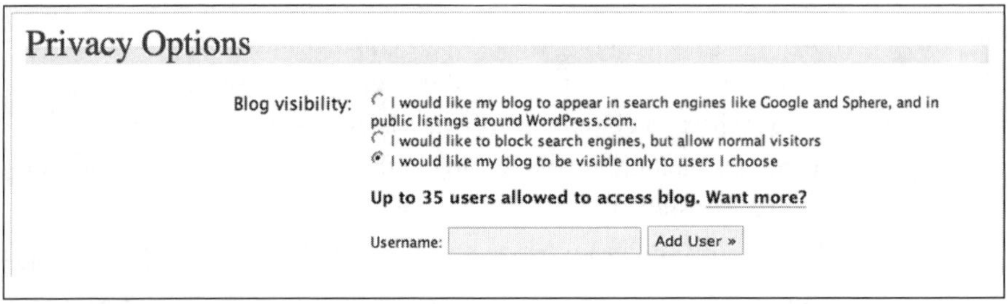

**Figure 3-2:** WordPress Privacy Options

The main advantage of a hosted solution is that it lifts the burden of support from local technology staff. This allows an organization to get a blog up and running in a very short amount of time without waiting for local technology support to install and configure software. Hosted solutions can also offer the advantages of built-in support, particularly if you are paying for a hosted solution. Many users also are more comfortable with hosted-solutions because they may have used them for a personal blog.

However, hosted solutions can have many downsides. First, hosted blogs may not be able to be highly customized in terms of look and feel. WordPress.com offers a limited number of free templates and plugins. Second, there is always a concern about backups and privacy of data with hosted solutions. Make sure you read the end-user license agreement before you put content up on a hosted blogging solution. Third, libraries may not be happy with the level of support provided by free hosted solutions. Check out the support options to make sure the company can meet your needs.

Another possible issue with hosted solutions is integrating the solution with existing authentication systems. Most hosted solutions won't let you use an existing store of usernames and passwords. This means blog authors will have a separate username and password to remember from the username and password that they use for most of their daily activities. Local IT will not be able to assist them if they forget their password, instead they will have to get their password reset via the hosted blogging software.

## Server-based Blogging Software

Server-based blogging solutions are typically run on local servers by local technology support. Some popular server-based blogging solutions include TextPattern, Community Server, WordPress, and Movable Type. Additionally, some content management systems such as Drupal can be used as server-based blogging solutions. Some server-based solutions are free and some are not. WordPress is a free and open source solution while Movable Type is open source but commercial and education licenses cost money.

The advantage of a server-based blogging solution is that it can be more extensively customized. This is particularly true for open source server-based solutions like WordPress. Not only can the look and feel of the blogs be customized, but the interface itself can be modified and extended.

The main disadvantage of a server-based solution is the fact that support burden is squarely on the shoulders of the local technology staff. With a small or nonexistent IT staff, this may be an unrealistic option. However, many of these open source packages are extremely easy to install and configure, and enthusiastic volunteers could do this work. Both LITA Blog and the code4lib blog/ Web site operate this way. The main technology support for the maintenance of the blog falls to a small group of volunteers.

In choosing which blogging solution is right for your project, you need to consider several factors. How much money do you have to spend? Do you have staff in-house capable and willing to support the blog? How many blogs are you going to run?

# CHAPTER 4

# *Hosted Blogs*

A hosted blog is one where the software running the blog runs somewhere other than your server, and many people use the same service for their blogs. A hosted blog solution is most like a Web-based e-mail account in form. You visit a Web site, give the site some information about yourself, and you have a blog.

There are some obvious advantages for this type of blog, the primary being that you have no software upkeep. You don't have to worry about upgrading, backing up, or any sort of maintenance—just type and go. The other advantage is that occasionally the larger hosted solutions (Blogger, for example) can manage to include services that no local install could, purely from the power of the size of the company. Since Blogger is owned by Google, it is capable of integrating on the backend of the software in ways that a locally hosted software would struggle to accomplish.

The biggest disadvantage of a hosted blogging solution is that you don't have as much control or customizability. You just can't dig into most hosted solutions in the same way you can server-based, and you are limited in how you can add things you wish to the blog. You are also at the mercy of the blog provider as to terms of use and the ability to get at your data if you ever decide to migrate your blog. Some systems (Blogger) are easy when it comes to these sorts of issues, while others (LiveJournal) are not.

Getting to your data can be a big deal. Therefore, if you are using a hosted service, it may be a good idea to keep a local backup copy of postings. Once more, using a big name provider has the advantage of having a big company behind it. Since Google isn't likely to go away soon, neither is your blog. You should keep this sort of thing in mind when you are deciding on the platform for your library.

# Blogger

Blogger <blogger.com> is a hosted service owned by Google and is one of the oldest hosted blogging sites on the Web. It is one of the most flexible of the hosted solutions, allowing a sort of hybrid hosted/server-based solution that involves using FTP to host just the HTML involved in the blog (don't worry if that sentence isn't completely clear, Blogger is talked about in detail later in the book).

Blogger is, in addition to being one of the most open and easy-to-use blogging services, free. A basic blog can be set up, hosted, and maintained at no cost through Blogger, which makes it perfect for initial forays into blogging, or for cash-strapped libraries.

# TypePad

TypePad <typepad.com> is the hosted blogging solution from Six Apart, the company that also produces Movable Type. TypePad is popular with professional bloggers, bloggers who actually earn a living through their writing online. This seems reasonable, since TypePad is one of a very few hosted blogging solutions that charge for access and ongoing use.

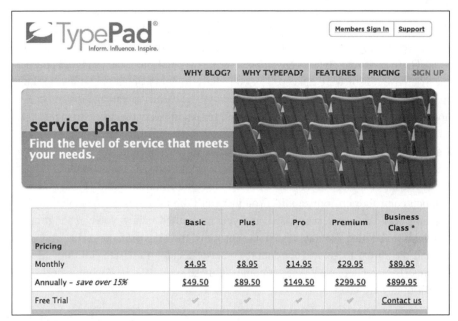

| | Basic | Plus | Pro | Premium | Business Class * |
|---|---|---|---|---|---|
| **Pricing** | | | | | |
| Monthly | $4.95 | $8.95 | $14.95 | $29.95 | $89.95 |
| Annually - *save over 15%* | $49.50 | $89.50 | $149.50 | $299.50 | $899.95 |
| Free Trial | ✓ | ✓ | ✓ | ✓ | Contact us |

**Figure 4-1:** Pricing for TypePad

TypePad is a powerful hosted solution and offers podcasting support, built-in photo albums, and other multimedia options not found in some other hosted options. The only real downside to TypePad is the ongoing cost, especially as it compares to Blogger and others. But libraries are used to this model of software where there are ongoing fees for maintenance and support, and having a more formal customer/client relationship with their provider may make adoption easier on the administration.

# LiveJournal

Livejournal <livejournal.com>, also a Six Apart product, is another free option for hosted blogging.

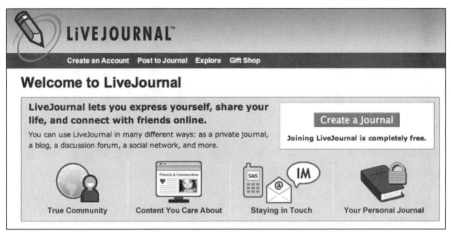

**Figure 4-2:** LiveJournal Home Page

It is more of a social-networking site than other hosted blogging solutions. It allows for friends to connect their blogs together and easily jump from one to the next in a more intuitive way than building a list of links for a traditional blog. LiveJournal also includes a group of services that don't come "out of the box" for other solutions, such as the ability to set up polls, do audio posts, and manage your photos. Like other Six Apart services, there are tiers of pricing for LiveJournal, with the basic service being free and additional services being a monthly charge.

LiveJournal has a reputation in the blogosphere as being primarily a social space rather than an informative one. The common perception is that it is far more like an actual online journal than a space for professional discussion, not that pro-fessional discussion isn't available. LiveJournal would be a good place for a school librarian to be if the students were using it extensively, although not likely for an academic librarian.

On December 3, 2007, it was announced that LiveJournal had been sold by Six Apart to SUP, an international media company based out of Moscow. SUP spun off a U.S.-based company, LiveJournal, Inc. to oversee the running of the service.

| Choose Account Level ▶ | Basic | Plus* | Paid |
|---|---|---|---|
| Pricing | FREE | **FREE** | **Starting under $2/mo*** |
| Display Userpics on Posts and Comments | 6 | **15** | **30** |
| Numerous Pre-made Designs for Your Journal | 100 | **300** | **600+** |
| Get Notified of New Posts, Friends, Comments, etc. | 25 | **200** | **1000** |
| Post Photos & Text via Your Mobile Device | | ⊘ | ⊘ |
| Get Free Text Message Notifications | | **3/mo** | **10/mo** |
| Create and Post Polls and Surveys | | ⊘ | ⊘ |
| Add Voice Posts (Audio Posts) to Your Journal | | **5/mo** | **20/mo** |
| Create Custom Mood Themes to Express a Mood | | ⊘ | ⊘ |
| Store and Manage Your Photos | | **1GB** | **2GB** |
| Point Your Personal URL to Your Journal (Domain Forwarding) | | ⊘ | ⊘ |
| Use the Advanced Search Options | | ⊘ | ⊘ |
| Earn Extra Userpics with Our Loyalty Program | | | ⊘ |
| Receive an @LiveJournal.com E-mail Address | | | ⊘ |
| Access the "Express Lane" for faster service during high traffic | | | ⊘ |
| Advertising Free | | | ⊘ |

**Figure 4-3:** Pricing for LiveJournal

# WordPress.com

WordPress.com is the hosted version of the WordPress blogging platform. WordPress is an open source software product, which means that the code is available for anyone to download, change, upgrade, or otherwise fiddle with. Since the point of a hosted solution is, largely, to avoid having to deal with code, WordPress.com is the perfect solution for someone who wants a hosted solution but still wants the flexibility that WordPress brings.

WordPress.com is free to use, and to sign up is a five-minute process. There is an "advanced" version of WordPress.com, but it doesn't add features to your experience, it is only for truly high traffic (more than 500,000 page-views a month) blogs.

WordPress.com, similarly to TypePad, has paid options. For WordPress.com, however, these are upgrades to the blog itself and not tiered pricing structures for differing levels of service. As an example, if you need extra space to store files for your blog (music, video, etc.) you can add one gigabyte of space for $20 a year. It costs $15 a year to add the ability to customize the CSS for your template on WordPress.com.

WordPress.com allows for a significant amount of customizing of your theme/template, on par with Blogger, and gives you many templates to choose from. The control panel for WordPress.com is nearly identical to the open source WordPress version, which is handy if you can see migrating at some point.

As a testament to how committed WordPress.com is to open source, the code that WordPress.com uses is a version of WordPress called WordPress MU (multi-user). That code is open as well, so if you have some technically savvy person that can set it up, you can host your own WordPress.com. That is, WordPress MU allows anyone to be a host for blogs. You can find information about WordPress MU at <http://mu.WordPress.com>.

## *Others*

There are a number of hosted blog solutions other than those specifically called out above, too many to fully enumerate here. There are three services that should be pointed out due to their specific focus on education blogging.

**Figure 4-4:** Edublogs.org

Edublogs.org is a WordPress MU-powered hosted solution that is tweaked and set up specifically for educational users. It is designed for teachers and administrators who wish to quickly step into a blog but may need some pedagogical suggestions about use of the platform. Librarians, especially school, public, and academic librarians who do instruction of any sort, could potentially benefit from this information. Edublogs is free for a basic account, with charges for more advanced options.

Another hosted service that librarians may find of benefit is called Class Blogmeister and can be found at <classblogmeister.com>. It was designed by David Warlick to answer some of the problems he saw with using other blog platforms for educational uses, primarily in the interactions between the students and the instructor. For example, Class Blogmeister includes the ability to grade student work (student posts) and manage those grades easily.

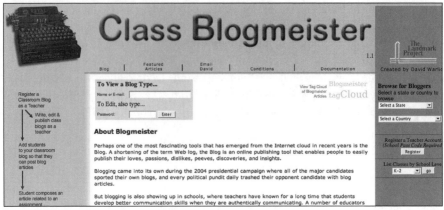

**Figure 4-5:** Class Blogmeister

The sign-up process appears to be a bit more involved than a generic hosted blog service, since Blogmeister wants to be able to categorize the blogs by grade and geographic location. You must first sign up for a school code and then use that code to register a teacher's account. After that, you are up and running.

Class Blogmeister is probably not the ideal platform for all types of library blogs, but it shows the detail to which a hosted solution can go in order to meet the needs for a specific group.

Another focused place to find a hosted blog solution specially designed for K-12 situations is ePals <www.epals.com>. ePals is a comprehensive solution for controlled communication in a K-12 setting. The strength of ePals is that it is designed with educational goals in mind and has strong audience limitation options (just your class, your class and another class, or combinations of types of users). ePals also makes it easy to link classes together and with its international user base, is potentially a revolutionary service for multicultural or foreign language study. The downside to ePals is that the interface, while attractive, isn't as straightforward as some of the less-complicated options on the Internet.

For the school librarian, ePals could be a useful option, especially for controlled, closed access to a blog for a specific class, but it doesn't fit the needs of the academic or public librarian in most cases. The ePals blogging service, called SchoolBlog, is free, as is its e-mail service.

Other services that fall under the general category of hosted blog service include MySpace, the popular social networking site <www.myspace.com> and Windows Live Spaces™ <spaces.live.com>, just to name a couple of the larger services. Any potential hosted service that your library may use would need to be carefully evaluated to ensure that it does what you want on a day-to-day basis and that the software is going to be around for you to continue to use. In this case, often bigger is better as far as the company you want standing behind your blogging efforts.

CHAPTER 5

# *Server-Based Blogging Solutions*

Server-based blogging solutions are typically run on local servers by local technology support. Some popular server-based blogging solutions include TextPattern, WordPress, and Movable Type. Additionally, some content management systems such as Drupal can be used as a server-based blogging solution. Some server-based solutions are free and some are not. WordPress is a free and open source solution while Movable Type is open source but charges for commercial/education licenses. Different server-based blogging solutions have different capabilities.

## *WordPress*

WordPress <www.wordpress.org> is an open source, server-based blogging solution that was originally developed in 2003. WordPress is designed to support a single blog, with one or many authors. WordPress is written in PHP and uses MySQL to store its data. WordPress creates a blog dynamically when a URL is requested, meaning that few actual pages reside on the server. WordPress blogs are highly customizable in terms of look and feel and also functionality. There are many WordPress templates available on the Web for people to download. Some of the best can be found at the WordPress Theme Viewer Web site <http://themes.WordPress.net/>. In terms of extensibility, developers have created numerous WordPress plugins. One place to find plugins is the WordPress plugin directory <http://WordPress.org/extend/plugins/>.

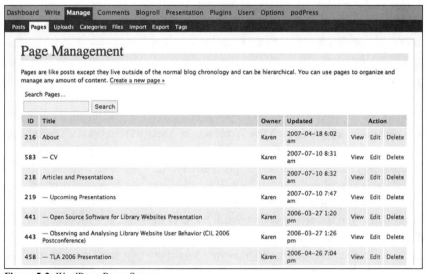

**Figure 5-1** WordPress Plugins Web Page

WordPress has many features that make it popular with bloggers. First, it contains a WYSIWYG editor that allows bloggers to easily format posts. Second, WordPress is extremely popular because it creates XHTML and CSS-standards compliant code. Third, WordPress has a Pages feature that allows bloggers to have regular Web pages as part of their blog with little coding effort. The Pages feature of WordPress allows a blog to be more like a regular Web site. Pages can be organized into a hierarchy, with sub-pages. This Pages functionality of WordPress makes the software a very simplistic content management system.

| ID | Title | Owner | Updated | Action | | |
|----|-------|-------|---------|--------|--|--|
| 216 | About | Karen | 2007-04-18 6:02 am | View | Edit | Delete |
| 583 | — CV | Karen | 2007-07-10 8:31 am | View | Edit | Delete |
| 218 | Articles and Presentations | Karen | 2007-07-10 8:32 am | View | Edit | Delete |
| 219 | — Upcoming Presentations | Karen | 2007-07-10 7:47 am | View | Edit | Delete |
| 441 | — Open Source Software for Library Websites Presentation | Karen | 2006-03-27 1:20 pm | View | Edit | Delete |
| 443 | — Observing and Analysing Library Website User Behavior (CIL 2006 Postconference) | Karen | 2006-03-27 1:26 pm | View | Edit | Delete |
| 458 | — TLA 2006 Presentation | Karen | 2006-04-26 7:04 pm | View | Edit | Delete |

**Figure 5-2:** WordPress Pages Screen

Like most blogs, WordPress also supports comments and trackbacks. Authors can control to which posts and pages users can add comments or trackbacks. To deal with comment spam, WordPress offers a number of options. First, WordPress allows you to moderate comments by requiring an e-mail address or a user who has posted a comment before. Second, a set of blacklist words can be configured. If a comment contains any of these words then it is sent to moderation. Also, the software includes a great spam catching plugin called Askimet. All of these options help to keep the amount of spam posted to a blog low.

Moderating comments means that the blog author needs to check the moderated comments queue to approve valid comments and delete spam comments. Doing this on a regular basis is essential so readers know their comments are being read.

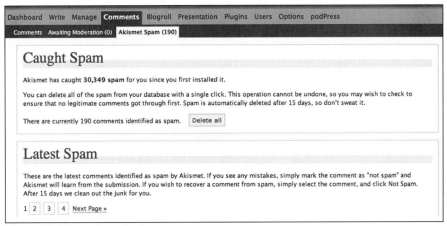

**Figure 5-3:** Akismet Spam Catcher

Another great feature of WordPress is the ability to assign different roles to different users of a WordPress blog. In WordPress, there are five different roles: Administrator, Editor, Author, Contributor, and Subscriber. Each role of user has a different set of permissions with Administrators having the most permissions and Subscribers the least. More information on WordPress roles can be found in the WordPress Codex <http://codex.WordPress.org/Roles_and_Capabilities#WordPress_Version_2.0>. This system of roles allows an administrator to granularly control what different users can do on a given blog. The LITA Blog uses this feature extensively because there currently are more than 500 users. While some of these users can publish content, others can only post content to be reviewed by users with editorial rights who will then review the content and publish it. WordPress' user roles allow easy manageability of these users by assigning them different permissions.

Another WordPress feature is the support for enclosures in RSS feeds. This means that WordPress can be used as a tool for podcasting. Additionally, WordPress has an upload tool that allows you to add multimedia content such as images, audio, and video to your blog. There are also plugins for embedding content from other media sites such as YouTube, Flickr, and Blip.tv. The best plugin for podcasting with WordPress is called Podpress and can be downloaded from <http://www.mightyseek.com/ podpress/>.

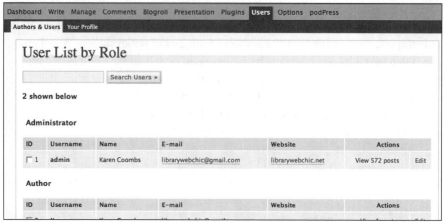

**Figure 5-4:** WordPress User Administration

As a blogging solution, WordPress has several strengths. It is extremely easy to install. The WordPress Web site offers a "5 Minute Installation Guide" for the tech savvy. For the less technically adept, a typical installation should take 15-20 minutes. Additionally, because all the aspects of a WordPress blog are dynamic, it is extremely scaleable. Creating a customized look and feel for your weblog is relatively simple using the templates. Moreover, WordPress is an extremely flexible tool that can be extended and modified to meet a variety of user needs. There is an extensive developer community that both maintains and updates the WordPress code. Bug fixes and updates are released on a regular basis.

The major disadvantage to WordPress as a blogging solution is that it doesn't come with built-in support. If something goes wrong you will be primarily reliant on the WordPress Forums and skills in-house to solve the problem. An additional concern is if you plan on running many blogs. WordPress is designed to run a single blog. If you want to run many blogs in a WordPress setup, you will need to check out WordPress MU <http://mu.WordPress.org> or Lyceum <http://lyceum. ibiblio.org> multiblog forks of WordPress. Currently, Harvard and Edublogs (seen in previous section) use WordPress MU to run their blogs.

# Movable Type

Movable Type <www.movabletype.com> is a server-based blogging solution that was originally developed in 2001 by the California-based company Six Apart. In contrast to WordPress, Movable Type is designed to support multiple blogs with one or many authors. Movable Type is written in Perl and can store its data in a variety of ways including SQLite, PostgreSQL, or MySQL databases. Movable Type blogs are typically created in a static fashion. However, portions of the blog can be generated in a dynamic fashion using PHP and Smarty templating as well. The personal version of Movable Type is free. However, commercial and educational licenses for Movable Type will vary in cost depending on the size of your organization.

Movable Type has a variety of features that make it a good server-based solution. Like WordPress the latest version has a WYSIWYG editor for composing content and allows users to create both posts and pages. It also can be extended using plugins <http://plugins.movabletype.org/> and customized using styles and templates <http://www.sixapart.com/movabletype/styles/index>.

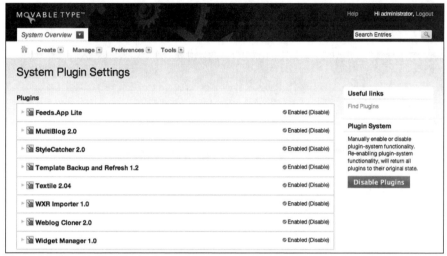

**Figure 5-5:** Movable Type Plugins Screen

Movable Type also allows blog readers to add comments or trackbacks to blog posts. Like WordPress, Movable Type allows you to choose whether or not to moderate comments. It includes a black list of words that automatically transfer a comment to the "to be moderated" queue. However, these settings are in the Plugins portion of the site rather than the comments Configuration section, which can make them more difficult to locate. Also, in the Plugins section is Movable Type's set of spam catcher plugins that can be configured to reduce spam comments.

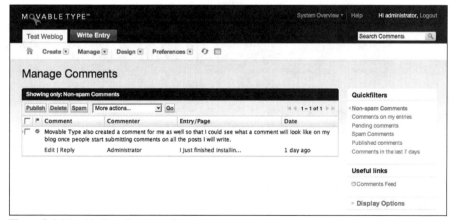

**Figure 5-6:** Movable Type Comments Screen

Movable Type has a robust user management system based on roles. Movable Type has eight pre-defined roles to which a user can be assigned: Author, Blog Administrator, Commentor, Contributor, Designer, Editor, Moderator, and Webmaster. Each of these roles can perform different tasks within Movable Type. Roles in Movable Type are assigned on a blog-by-blog basis. Therefore, User A may be an Editor on Blog 1 but only a Contributor on Blog 2. In addition, Movable Type allows you to create new roles. This is very helpful if you need different granularity of permissions than the pre-defined roles provide.

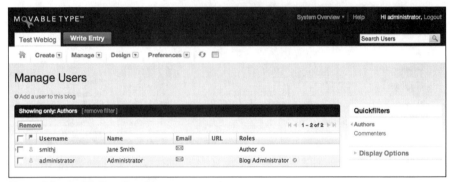

**Figure 5-7:** Movable Type User Management

In addition to the basic functions that it shares with other blog software, Movable Type has some unique functionality as well. It offers an asset management system for managing media like images, audio, and video. Movable Type also includes integrated e-mail notifications, which allows you to let your readers know when a thread has been updated. Another important feature is that it can be used to centrally manage several blogs and users. A part of this is blog cloning, which is the ability to create a new blog that inherits the styles, settings, templates, and configuration of any blog in your system. For an organization running many blogs this is crucial to creating blogs with a consistent look and feel. Movable Type also creates dynamic charts showing recent commenting and posting activity.

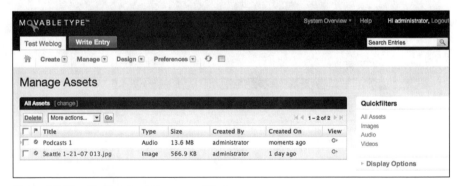

**Figure 5-8:** Movable Type Asset Management Feature

Moreover, Movable Type blends the best of open source software with commercial support options. The code for Movable Type is available to developers via an open source GPL license. However, because Movable Type is a commercial product, Six Apart offers more support options for purchase. For example, if you are uncomfortable with installing software on a Web server, you can purchase installation service from Six Apart.

Movable Type has several strengths. First, it can support many blogs with multiple authors in a scaleable fashion. Second, it offers several support options for organizations with small technology staff. Additionally, there is a good developer and user community surrounding Movable Type. This includes users who are creating personal blogs as well as large organizations using Movable Type to support hundreds of blogs. In fact, many universities including the University of British Columbia, University of Saskatchewan, and Case Western University use Movable Type to support their university weblogs. The University of Minnesota Libraries uses Movable Type for the UThink project, which provides blogs to students, faculty, and staff on campus.

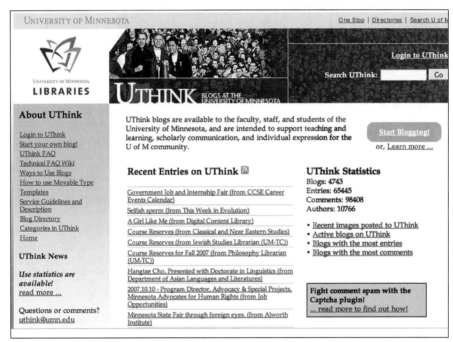

**Figure 5-9:** UThink Project Web Site

Movable Type has weaknesses as well. The chief of these being that the primary publishing model for Movable Type is static HTML pages, which take up server space. While Movable Type can operate in a dynamic fashion, many plugins cannot be used with dynamic templates. The static page creation model of Movable Type also has another problem: making changes to templates can become a tedious process across a static blog. This is because every file may need to be updated. Once a blog contains more than a few entries or you have multiple blogs, rebuilding becomes very time consuming.

# Others

In addition to WordPress and Movable Type, there are several other server-based blogging solutions. Some of these are blogging software, while others are more true content management systems.

In the realm of blogging software there are a plethora of open source server-based options. Included in this list are Lyceum, Subtext, and Typo. Like WordPress, all these systems have the standard pitfalls and strengths of free open source software. The user/developer community around these systems is smaller than the WordPress community, and as a result, the support options limited. However, if your library only runs software written in a specific language, one of these systems might suit your needs. Lyceum utilizes the WordPress blogging engine at its core. However, Lyceum is capable of supporting multiple blogs. Subtext <http://subtextproject.com/> uses ASP.NET with a Microsoft SQL database. Subtext can support multiple blogs within the same instance. Typo, <www.typosphere.org> uses the Ruby on Rails™ framework with a MySQL, PostgreSQL, or SQLite database. It has nice widgets that allow you to easily customize the sidebar of your blog.

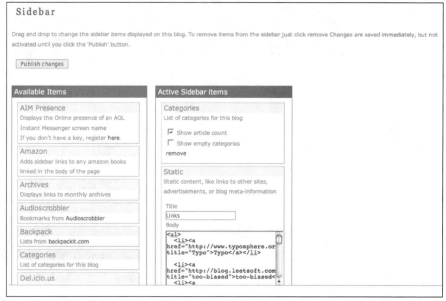

**Figure 5-10:** Typo Sidebar Widgets

Of these options Lyceum is likely your best choice if you want an open source system capable of supporting multiple blogs and users. If you want to try something new and bleeding edge, Typo may be more up your alley.

Several open source content management systems also offer blogging functionality. Content management systems are designed to manage the content of an entire Web site. This content can be traditional Web pages, event calendars, or blogs. The most notable open source CMS with blogging functionality are

Textpattern and Drupal. Textpattern <http://textpattern.com/> uses PHP with a MySQL database. A few libraries are using Textpattern for blogging purposes. However, in most instances it seems to be the tool of choice because the library is managing its Web site with Textpattern. This is the case with the Mosman Library in Australia <http://www.mosman.nsw.gov.au/library>. Another example of a Textpattern powered library Web site and blog is the Madison-Jefferson County Public Library in Indiana <http://www.mjcpl.org/?s=Library-Buzz>.

**Figure 5-11:** Madision Jefferson County Public Library Blog

Drupal <http://drupal.org/> uses PHP with a MySQL or PostgreSQL database. There are library blogs being run on Drupal. In fact, Ann Arbor District Library in Michigan uses Drupal for both its blogs and its entire library Web site. The University of Calgary and the University of Prince Edward Island both use Drupal to run blogs for their universities. However, Drupal can be slightly intimidating to implement. Therefore, think carefully about choosing this software. If your blogs aren't part of a larger Web site that you want to manage with content management system, Drupal or any other content management system may be an inappropriate choice.

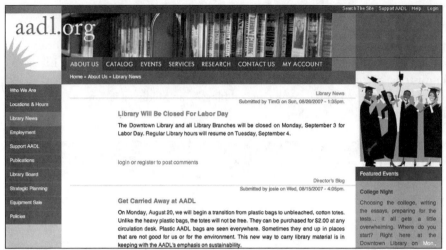

**Figure 5-12:** Ann Arbor District Library Web Site

# INSTRUCTIONS/ HOW TO SECTION

CHAPTER 6

# *Wordpress.com How To*

WordPress.com is a hosted blogging services that relies on a modified version of the popular open source blogging software WordPress <www.wordpress.org>. WordPress.com has many of the same features as the server-based version of WordPress. Users can create Posts, Pages, and Categories. Comments can be submitted to WordPress.com blogs, and the site has an excellent spam-catching program called Akismet. The service allows for each blog to have multiple authors with permissions ranging from contributor to administrator. Additionally, the look and feel of blogs can be customized using one of the more than 40 themes that WordPress.com has installed. The header image and header text can be altered to further customize the blog. However, if you want to make changes to the cascading style sheet then you will need to pay an upgrade fee. The sidebar can be tailored using "sidebar widgets" for external services like del.icio.us, Meebo, and Flickr.

WordPress.com blogs can be made "private" so that only authorized users can visit them. Private blogs serve a variety of purposes. They can be used to do collaborative type work that you only want a particular group of people to see, such as internal communications or testing. Making a blog private is also a good way for an organization or individual to work on building a blog in private then debut the finished product to the world.

WordPress.com comes with a full-featured rich text editor with inline spell-checker that makes it easy to create posts. Additionally, the service allows you to upload your own photos or include images from other services such as Flickr. There is also the ability to embed videos from YouTube or GoogleVideo and audio from Odeo (a podcasting service). Wordpress.com offers a built-in auto-save mechanism that keeps you from losing work in the event of computer crash or other potential errors. WordPress.com also offers real-time statistics on who is visiting your blog, which posts are the most popular, what search terms are sending people to your blog, and how many people are subscribed to your feed. A tool like this is not available in Blogger. In the case of server-based blogging tools, this is typically an add-on that you or your host would need to run.

The major advantage of WordPress.com is the user support that comes with the standard service. There is an excellent FAQ and many support forums as well as a form where you can contact support directly to assist you with problems.

One limitation of WordPress.com and all hosted blogging options is that you can't extend the functionality of the software the way you can with an open source server-based product like WordPress. However, WordPress.com has forms available that allow users to request new features and a Web forum specifically related to ideas and suggestions. If these features are not necessary for your blog, then WordPress.com is a good solution if you can't or don't want to run blogging software yourself.

## Setting Up a WordPress.com Weblog

If you want to have a blog at WordPress.com then the first thing you need to do is sign up for an account. You can do this by visiting the WordPress.com site <http://www.WordPress.com> and clicking on the Get a WordPress Blog Now link. This will take you to a screen where you are asked to select a username and fill in your e-mail address. Make sure you read the terms of service, particularly the "Responsibility of Contributors" section, which outlines what you may and may not do on your WordPress.com blog.

You will be then asked to choose a name for your blog, a URL for your blog at WordPress.com, the language your blog is in, and whether or not you want your blog to be publicly available.

Once you fill out this form, an e-mail message asking you to activate your account will be sent to the e-mail address you supplied when you created your account. Click on the Active link to activate your blog. After you have done this, another e-mail with your account username, password, and your blog URL will be sent to you.

**Figure 6-1:** WordPress Account Creation Form

**Figure 6-2:** WordPress Blog Creation Form

**Figure 6-3:** WordPress Login Screen

Go to your blog's login page and use your username and password to login.

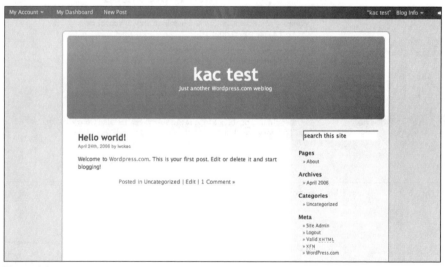

**Figure 6-4:** Sample WordPress Blog Home

This will log you into your blog and take you to your blog home page.

From here, click on the My Dashboard link, which will take you to the main administrative screen for your blog from which you can create new posts, pages,

**Figure 6-5:** WordPress Blog Administration

and customize your blog.

# Customizing the Look and Feel

Once you've created a blog account for yourself, the first thing you will want to do is customize the look and feel of your blog. Under the Presentations link, there are a number of tools to change the layout and design of your blog. The most important of these is the theme selection tool. This tool lets you choose from more than 40 preset themes that create an overall look for your blog. Examine the thumbnails of the different themes and choose the one that fits you and your blog best. Don't worry if you select a theme and then decide you don't like it. You can change the

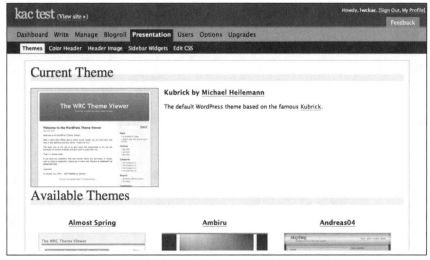

**Figure 6-6:** WordPress Theme Selection

theme of your blog at any time, so feel free to try different things.

In addition to choosing a theme, you can also customize your blog by customizing the theme's header. How much you can alter the header varies from theme to theme. Some changes you can make to the header, depending on the theme, include changing the color and image of your header. The options for the different themes will appear at the top of the screen in the Presentation menu. In the default WordPress.com theme, for example, you can use the Color Header and Header Image links to change the color of the text within the header, the background color on which it sits, and the image used in your header.

In many themes (including the default), you can use the Sidebar Widgets option to customize the sidebar of your blog. To customize your sidebar, click on the Sidebar Widgets link. Next, drag and drop the widgets you want to include in your sidebar into the sidebar box. Finally, click the Save Changes button to save your customized sidebar. In the example below, sidebar widgets were used to customize the sidebar of the blog so that it has a search box for the blog, links to previous posts in the blog archives, a link to the blog's RSS feed, a del.icio.us

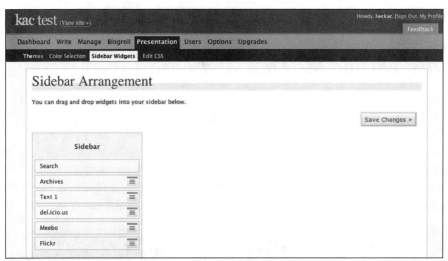

**Figure 6-7:** WordPress Sidebar Customization

linklog, a link to Meebo for chat, and recent Flickr photos.

Most external services that you can add to your sidebar require some configuration. For example, you must input your del.icio.us username to get the linklog to display properly. There are good directions with the WordPress administrative tool on how to get the information you need to make the widgets work. If you have difficulties, check the Forums or use the Contact Support link. One item that you will probably want to add to your sidebar is a link to the blog's RSS feed. The steps for doing this are not intuitive, so they have been added here. First, drag and drop a Text Widget into your sidebar where you want the link to the RSS feed to appear. Next click the Configure button in the Text Widget. This will pop open a little window where you want to paste the following code:

<a href="<http://blogname.WordPress.com/feed>"><img

src="'<http://faq.WordPress.com/files/2006/07/button_rss.gif' alt=""RSS"" /></a>

Remember to change "blogname.WordPress.com" to your blog's URL. Close the window and click the Save Changes button. This will generate the RSS 2.0 image and a link to the blog's RSS feed. Examining the public view of this blog, a user will see that the sidebar includes all of these items in the sidebar. Some other helpful items you can add to your sidebar include statistics for your blog, links to all the pages that are part of your blog, RSS feed items from an external site, and text links to other Web pages. Be careful using sidebar widgets with different themes as the appearance of the sidebar may change greatly when you change the theme. Make sure if you change your theme to check the sidebar is displaying properly after the change.

# Pointers for Posting

WordPress.com includes a very simple and easy to use WYSIWYG editor for creating blog posts. With the editor you can easily create and format text. The editor has buttons for making lists, inserting images, adding links, and centering text. The edi-

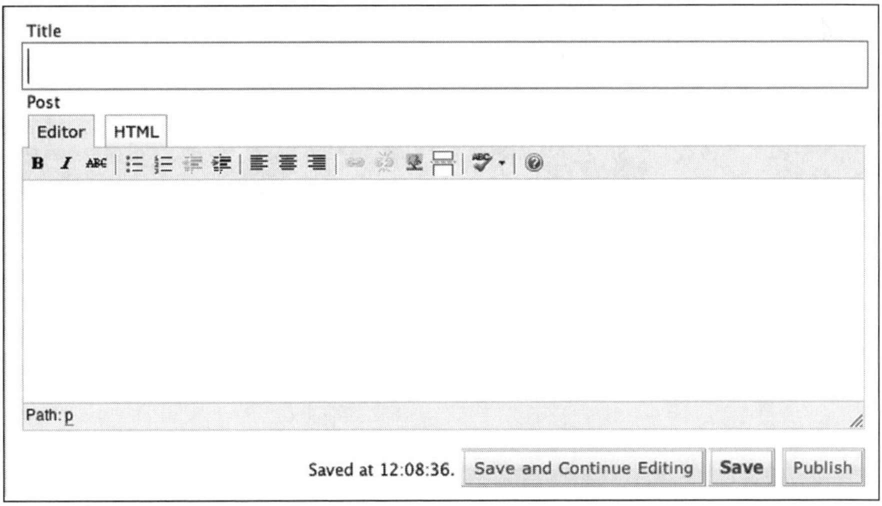

**Figure 6-8:** WordPress WYSIWYG Editor

tor also includes a spell-checking utility.

In addition, you can add different types of multimedia to your blog. This includes photos from Flickr or ones that you upload, video from YouTube or Google Video, and audio from Odeo. To upload photos to your blogs, use the

**Figure 6-9:** WordPress File Upload Step 1

Upload tab within the post composition page.

Browse the files on your computer to locate the photo you want to upload. Select this photo then click the Upload button. You will then be asked if you want to link to a file or a page. Choose file and click Send to Editor. This will add the photo to the editor. If the photo isn't the correct size you can resize it using the WordPress editor. This can be difficult so it is more efficient to make sure the pic-

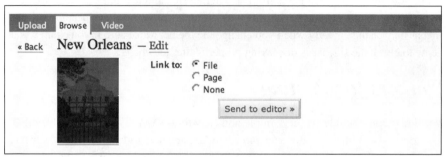

**Figure 6-10:** WordPress File Upload Step 2

ture is the size you want it to be before you upload it.

If you already have a photo in Flickr you want to use in your blog, then you need to click the image button to link to this photo. This will pop up a window

| ✕ | Insert/edit image |
| --- | --- |

Insert/edit image

Image URL

Image description

Alignment     -- Not set --

Dimensions     ☐ × ☐

Border     ☐

Vertical space     ☐

Horizontal space     ☐

Cancel                                                                 Insert

**Figure 6-11:** WordPress Image Popup Window

where you need to put in the URL to the photo on Flickr.

You can get the URL for the Flickr photo by navigating to the photo's page in Flickr, then using the All Sizes link to view all the photo sizes. Clicking on the different size photos will give you a URL, which you can cut and paste into the image

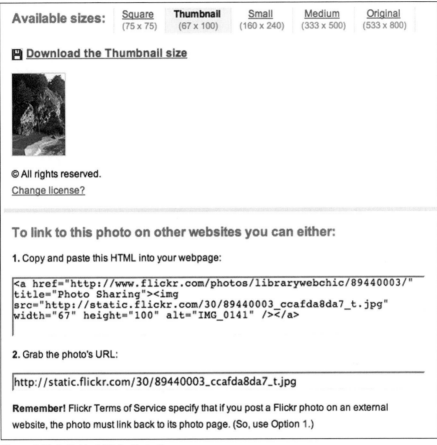

**Figure 6-12:** Individual Flickr Photo Screen

popup.

Videos can also be added using Web-based video services. For example you can upload a video to YouTube and then link to it in your blog. To do this, login to YouTube, click on the Home tab then the Videos link. Here you will see an Upload Video button. Click on this and fill in the basic information about your video. Click the Continue button which will take you to a screen where you can browse your local hard drive for the video you want to upload. Choose the desired video and

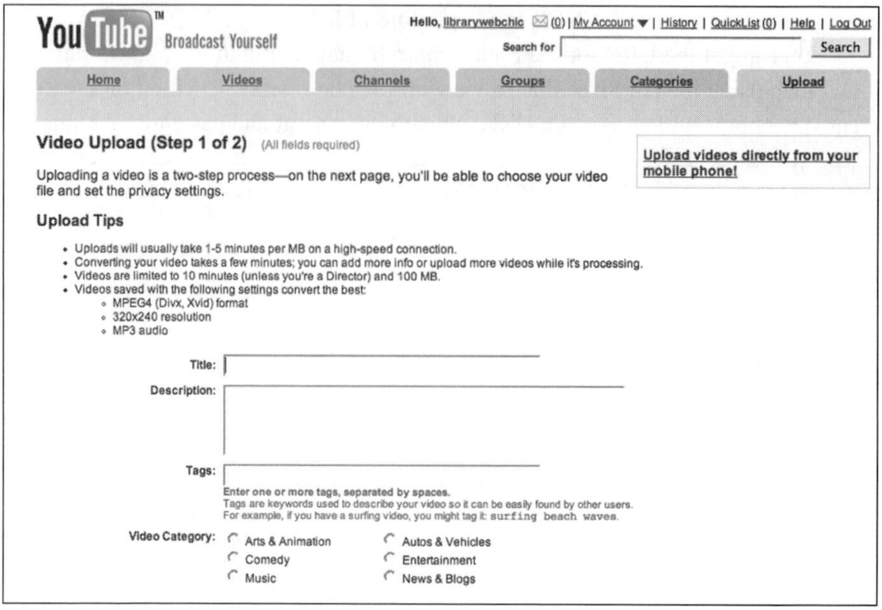

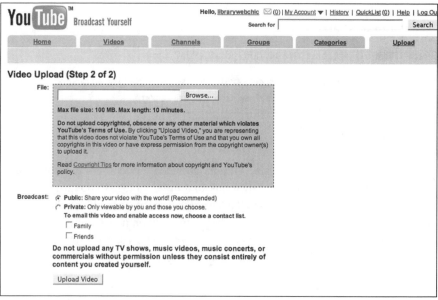

**Figure 6-13:** YouTube Upload Step 1

click the Upload Video button.

Because of its size, it will take some time to upload your video. When the upload is complete, you will see a message that indicates that the video has been

**Figure 6-14:** YouTube Upload Step 2

successfully uploaded. In this same screen will be a URL for your video.

Copy the URL and put that between [youtube= and] to make [youtube= http://www.youtube.com/watch?v=K9cBQU6kVfw]. Then insert this code into the WordPress post.

Additionally, you can use your blog to distribute audio content in the form of a podcast. WordPress.com allows you to distribute content via Odeo, a Web-based podcasting service. To do this, go to the audio from Odeo you want to embed in

**Figure 6-15:** Odeo Audio File Screen

your blog.

Then copy and paste the URL in your address bar; it should look like this: [http://odeo.com/audio/2171601/view]. Insert the URL into the WordPress.com editor by formatting it like this [odeo=http://odeo.com/audio/2171601/view]. Save the post, and the audio will be added.

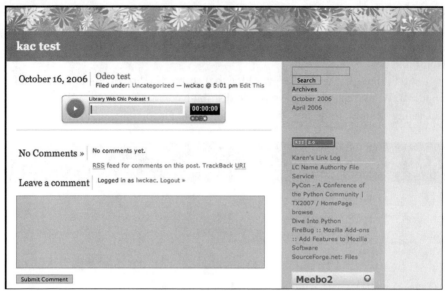

**Figure 6-16:** WordPress Blog with Odeo Audio Added to a Post

# CHAPTER 7

# *Blogger How To*

## *Introduction*

In August of 1999, the site Blogger.com was launched by a company called Pyra Labs. Blogger very quickly became the most popular hosted blog solution in the world, and in 2003 Blogger was purchased by Google. With Google's backing, a number of paid features became available for free, and Blogger continued to be a central destination for individuals and businesses wanting a quick blogging solution.

Blogger was the first to make signing up for a blog as easy as signing up for an online e-mail account. Simply enter a few pieces of information, choose a name and password, and you're off and running. The simplicity of getting started doesn't mean that the service itself is simple. Blogger provides users with many rich features that allow for customization and integration with lots of other Web 2.0 services around the web.

# Setting up a Blogger Weblog

**Figure 7-1:** Blogger Home Page

If you visit Blogger, you'll be faced with a friendly page that details the steps needed to get your blog started.

**Figure 7-2:** Blogger Account Creation Screen

Since Google purchased Blogger, it has integrated their single-login for other Google services into Blogger signup. By signing up for Blogger, you are in effect creating a Google login. All you need to do is enter an e-mail address, choose a password (eight characters minimum), enter the name you want associated with the posts, and enter a CAPTCHA to ensure you are really a human. Then click Continue.

**Figure 7-3:** Blogger Blog Creation Screen

On this next page, you have some important decisions to make. What is the name of your blog? What do you want your URL to be? Remember that the URL is important on the Web. It should be as short as possible and still recognizable as indicative of your library or group. You want people to be able to remember it, and you want it to be easily typed into an address bar. The name of the blog is important as it will be indexed by Google and other search engines and will be a primary way that patrons find your blog if they don't come directly from your library home page.

This is also the page where, if you have a local Web server where you want the blog to reside (not the software...just the HTML of the blog itself), you can go to the Advanced tab and set up the FTP information telling Blogger where to put the files. Blogger can be an excellent choice for school or public libraries since they often have Web sites, but the server involved may not be the newest and fastest and they may not be capable of running WordPress or other installed blogging options. With Blogger, you can set up the FTP option and have the blog live on your own Web server without the overhead of PHP or MySQL installation.

Once you've chosen a name and a URL, the next step is to choose a template for your blog. This is the look or theme of the blog, and it can be changed later or customized as you need. All of the built-in templates that Blogger uses are similar in basic structure and are composed of a header (top banner) and two columns (a main column and a sidebar).

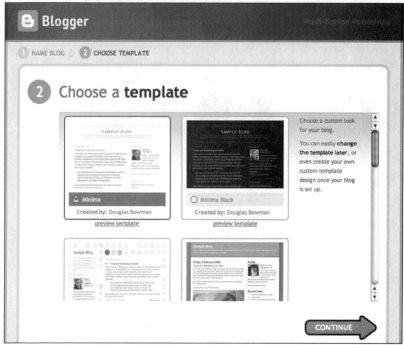

**Figure 7-4:** Blogger Select a Template

**Figure 7-5:** Blogger Blog Created Screen

That's it! You now have a blog. Blogger immediately provides you with its "posting" interface, allowing you to starting writing your first blog post.

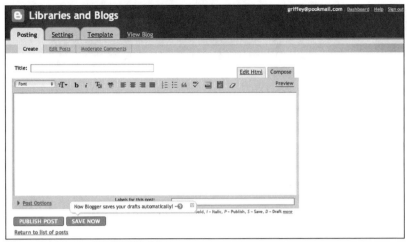

**Figure 7-6:** Blogger WYSIWYG Editor

If you look at the detail on the text entry area, you can see that it has very basic text editing abilities built-in: bold, italic, text color, the ability to make a hyperlink, and basic ordered and unordered lists are a push-button away. Type something and hit Publish, and it is added to your blog.

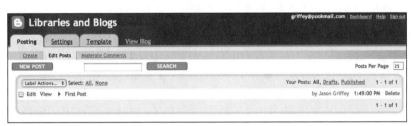

**Figure 7-7:** Blogger Edit Posts Screen

In addition to adding to your blog via posting, You have a link to Edit Posts and Moderate Comments on the same page as the text input area. Edit Posts allows you to go back in your timeline and change or delete old posts.

Moderate Comments allows you to edit or delete comments that others have left on your blog. This is very important for school or public library blogs that might cater to minors, as being able to moderate allows for a more controlled conversational space on the blog.

**Figure 7-8:** Blogger Settings Screen

The Settings tab is where all of the administrative instruments for the blog live and where you can change everything from the name of the blog to who can post to the blog. Under the Permissions link you can add multiple authors to a single blog, so you could have multiple members of your staff or faculty posting to the blog. You can also control such aspects of the blog as how many posts you want on the front page and how often you want Blogger to archive your posts. For a simple blog, you can more or less ignore most of the options in Settings, but if you want to stretch your customization of the blog, this is a good place to start.

## Customizing the Look and Feel

The final tab in the Blogger interface is the Template area, where you can customize not only how your blog looks but also add modules that tie your blog to other Web applications. Blogger provides the ability to add modules to your page (Google refers to these as Page Elements).

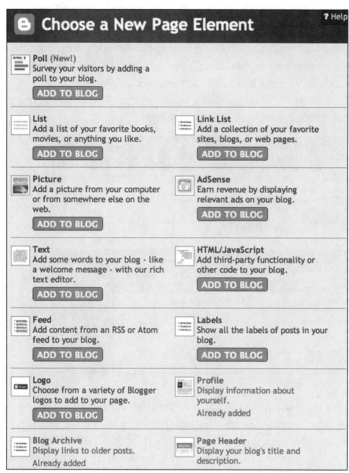

**Figure 7-9:** Blogger Add Page Elements

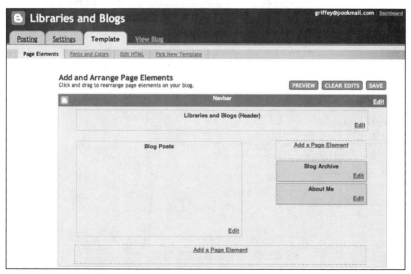

**Figure 7-10:** Blogger Arrange Page Elements

By simply clicking Add a Page Element you are given a screen similar to the above, where you can choose to add a picture, an RSS feed, or even a poll to your page. Rearranging these elements is as easy as dragging and dropping them into the order you want. The elements are flexible enough that nearly any RSS feed could be added to your blog, which means that nearly any content on the Web these days could be placed in your sidebar: del.icio.us links, Flickr photos, Twitter posts. You name the RSS feed, and Blogger will put it on your sidebar.

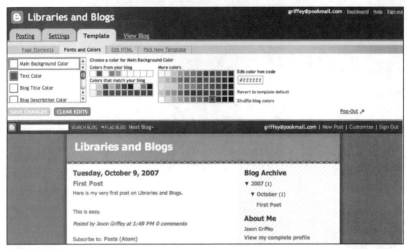

**Figure 7-11:** Customize Blogger Template Colors

Blogger also gives you complete control over the color scheme of your blog through an incredibly intuitive choose-and-click interface. You choose the element on the page you want to change: background color, text color, link color. Click the color you want it to be, and you're done. Blogger even gives you a palette of colors that are complimentary to the current theme, so you can tweak without clashing.

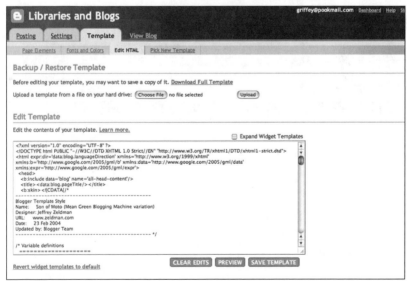

**Figure 7-12:** Edit Blogger Template

If you come to the blog table with pre-existing HTML talent, Blogger even lets you change your template directly by editing the HTML itself.

Using this interface you can modify your template directly, preview it, save the template HTML to your local machine for editing, or upload an existing template you've prepared. If something becomes messed up in your edits, you can simply choose a new template from the Blogger choices and you're right back in business.

# Semi-Hosted

Blogger has two further features that set it apart from the hosted blog competition. Blogger is the only hosted blogging solution that allows you to use the blogging software running on remote servers to update HTML that lives locally on your servers. The only requirement for this is to have FTP or SFTP access to the directory you wish the blog to live in on your server. The setup page looks like this:

**Publishing via FTP**

Switch to: • blogspot.com (Blogger's free hosting service) • Custom Domain (Point your own registered domain name to your blog) • SFTP (secure your ISP server)

| | | |
|---|---|---|
| **FTP Server** | | |
| | Example: yourwebsite.com | |
| **Blog URL** | | |
| | The web address where this blog is viewable without the filename (e.g. index.html). This should include http://. librariesandblogs.blogspot.com will redirect to your FTP blog. | |
| **FTP Path:** | | |
| | This path must already exist on your server. | |
| **Blog Filename:** | index.html | |
| | Example: index.html Warning: If this file already exists on your server in the path entered above, it will be OVERWRITTEN. Be sure to back it up. | |
| **Feed Filename:** | atom.xml | |
| | Example: atom.xml Warning: If this file already exists on your server in the path entered | |

**Figure 7-13:** Blogger Set Up External Web Server

If you fill out the information as asked, Google will re-publish your blog into the specified directory every time it is updated. This is the perfect solution if you have space on your Web server and want to be able to control the URL that your patrons access to get to your blog.

The second feature that makes Blogger an excellent choice for libraries is that even if you don't have a Web server sitting in a back closet that you can FTP into, you can still use a custom URL for your blog.

From this page, you can purchase a domain name directly from Google for $10. For your money, you not only get a custom URL for your blog, but Google will also redirect people from your blogspot.com address if you are upgrading and include

**Figure 7-14:** Purchase a Domain Name via Blogger

Google Apps for your domain so you get e-mail, document creation, and other Google services linked to your new URL. This custom URL via Blogger is a huge bargain for the library looking to spread its wings with a new sort of Web presence.

Blogger is definitely a great option for libraries looking for a fast and easy blogging solution. The real strength in Blogger is the options that you have in making it work just as you want it to. The disadvantages are that if you aren't familiar with HTML you are stuck with a reasonably small number of templates. Additionally, the URL matters when people are deciding what to trust online. If you stick with the .blogspot.com URL you risk alienating a subset of your users. But if you FTP your content or purchase a URL from Google, Blogger can be the perfect choice for the busy library to dive into blogging.

CHAPTER 8

# WordPress How To

While we've discussed many different blogging options, if you have the capacity to install and run WordPress, it is your best option for being able to customize your blog. In Chapter 5 we discussed WordPress, and here we will walk through how to install the open source WordPress on your own server. After the install, we'll look at installing themes, plugins, and other customizations.

There are two basic requirements for a web server to run the current version of WordPress (at the time of writing, version 2.3.1): PHP 4.2 and MySQL 4.0 or higher. You need to create a database for WordPress to use in your MySQL installation and remember the database name, username, and password that accesses it.

You should then download the latest version of WordPress from <http://wordpress.org/download/>. Most people should download the zipped version of the software. Unzip it on your computer, and open the resulting folder.

There are lots of files and a few folders in the resulting folder. We are interested in only one of them: `wp-config-sample.php`. A few lines in this file need to be edited before the file can be uploaded to your server. Open the file in a text editor such as Notepad on a Windows machine. Don't use Microsoft Word™ or another document editor for this, since they could unintentionally introduce hidden characters into the file that could cause problems when it is uploaded. When the file is opened, you'll see several lines of code that looks like this:

```
<?php

// ** MySQL settings ** //
define('DB_NAME', 'putyourdbnamehere');      // The name of the database
define('DB_USER', 'usernamehere');       // Your MySQL username
define('DB_PASSWORD', 'yourpasswordhere'); // ...and password
define('DB_HOST', 'localhost');      // 99% chance you won't need to
change this value
define('DB_CHARSET', 'utf8');
define('DB_COLLATE', '');

// You can have multiple installations in one database if you give
each a unique prefix
$table_prefix = 'wp_';    // Only numbers, letters, and underscores
please!
```

There are four lines in which we are interested. The first three lines under the MySQL settings entry should be changed to reflect the name of your database and the username and password associated with it. For example, if your database was named "betsy" and your username and password were "eliza" and "121507," the resulting wp-config-sample.php file would look like:

```
<?php

// ** MySQL settings ** //
define('DB_NAME', 'betsy);      // The name of the database
define('DB_USER', 'eliza');       // Your MySQL username
define('DB_PASSWORD', '121507'); // ...and password
```

The only other line that we could consider changing is the table prefix line.

```
// You can have multiple installations in one database if you give
each a unique prefix
$table_prefix = 'wp_';    // Only numbers, letters, and underscores
please!
```

If you wanted to manage multiple blogs using the same database, you could do so by making the prefix unique for each install of WordPress. If you think you will only want one blog using this database, you don't have to worry about the prefix. If you want to run multiple blogs you should probably be thinking about running one of the multiple-blog variants like Wordpress MU or Lyceum. For most users, you can leave this setting alone.

Once those changes have been made to the file, the file name needs to be changed. Just remove the "sample" from the name, so that the file is named `wp-config.php`. This file will tell WordPress how to connect to the database where it will store all of the information for your blog.

Now that we have the changes to wp-setup done, we can upload the files. Choose the directory on your server where you want your blog to reside, and upload the contents of the WordPress download to your server. There are several ways to get the files from your local computer to your server with the most common being via FTP or SFTP. Once all of the files have finished uploading, you're ready to install.

Open a Web browser, and in the address bar type in the location of your WordPress install, like this:

```
<http://www.yourwebsite.com/wp-admin/install.php>
```

Enter the URL of the location of the uploaded files, and append `/wp-admin/install.php` to it. That should bring you to the WordPress install page:

Welcome to WordPress installation. We're now going to go through a few steps to get you up and running with the latest in personal publishing platforms. You may want to peruse the ReadMe documentation at your leisure.

**First Step »**

**Figure 8-1:** WordPress Install Page

You should be able to click the Install button. That's it. If the MySQL settings were entered correctly, you should see this page:

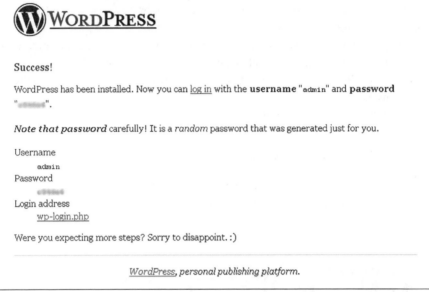

**Figure 8-2:** WordPress Successfully Installed

WordPress is that easy to install. You will see your login and password on the resulting screen, and you should copy that password to a text file or write it down so you don't forget it. Click the login link, and enter your login and password to get to the administration screen for your blog. Once you get to that point, you can change the password to something that is easier to remember.

On the administration screen, you will see a number of tabs that will allow you to control nearly every aspect of your blog. Because WordPress is an open source product, anyone can look at its code and write extensions for it. The two most common types of extensions are themes to change the look and feel of your blog, and plugins that allow for the extension of the capabilities of WordPress. If you search, you will find thousands of themes and plugins for WordPress. The process of installing them is similar to uploading the software in the first place; download the theme or plugin, unzip it if is is zipped, and then upload the files or folder to the appropriate folder on the server.

That place is:

For themes: /wp-content/themes

For plugins: /wp-content/plugins

Under the administration screen, there is a tab called Presentations. That tab will allow you to change the look of your blog to any of the installed themes by simply clicking on the theme you like. If you are familiar with and comfortable editing CSS, you can change many things about the theme by editing the CSS file associated with it. If you aren't comfortable with that, it isn't a problem; there are thousands of themes to choose from. You will definitely find one that you like.

Before you upload any plugin, you should carefully read any installation instructions to make sure that the version of WordPress that you are using is compatible with the plugin. Some plugins have slightly varied installation, depending on the complexity of the plugin. For most plugins, just uploading them to the correct folder is enough to get them in the correct place. After uploading, they need to be activated in the Plugin tab of the administration screen.

There is the small chance that, even after checking versions, a plugin may not work as advertised. In very rare cases, it may even cause your blog to not render properly. If this happens, fixing it is as easy as deleting the plugin from the directory. That will turn it off and remove any problems that it caused. Don't be worried about plugins. With WordPress you can't destroy your blog using them, even if one breaks badly.

Far more customizations and plugins exist for WordPress than could possibly be covered in a single chapter. Look around online for additional tutorials about customization, plugins, and other ways of making WordPress the system you want it to be.

Just after this manuscript was completed, Wordpress 2.5 was released, which changed some of the look and feel of the software. We will post any significant changes in the software to the blog for this book, which can be found at <http://www.libraryblogging.com>.

CHAPTER 9

# *Movable How To*

Movable Type is a server-based blogging program, which was developed by Six Apart. Movable Type is free for a single personal blog. However, educational institutions must license the commercial version of Movable Type. The commercial version of Movable Type comes with technical support, which the personal, free version lacks. Movable Type is written in Perl, and supports storage of the weblog's content and associated data within MySQL, PostgreSQL, and SQLite databases.

Movable Type supports both static and dynamic page generation. Static pages are recreated and updated when the content of the site is changed. In contrast, dynamic pages are created on the fly when the browser requests them, using the Smarty templating. Blog owners can choose to make their whole blog statically or dynamically generated. However, most Movable Type blogs contain both dynamic and static pages. Dynamic pages are typically used for pages whose content changes often. In contrast, static pages are often used for pages that aren't frequently updated.

One of the main advantages of Movable Type as a blogging platform is that it is capable of supporting multiple blogs that have multiple authors while WordPress is only capable of supporting a single blog. Movable Type has many features in common with other blogging software such as WordPress. Users can create blog posts and categories. Additionally, Movable Type includes the ability for users to add tags to their blog posts. Comments can be submitted to Movable Type weblogs, and Movable Type includes a basic spam-catching application.

The look and feel of blogs can be customized using templates, and widgets and by selecting a design with StyleCatcher. Like WordPress, Movable Type's functionality can be extended using plugins. Another important feature is the Notification List. The Notification List is a set of e-mail addresses in Movable Type that can be e-mailed when a post is updated.

Unlike previous versions of Movable Type, Movable Type 4 comes with a WYSIWYG editor. This functionality is a major improvement over previous versions where users had to install a plugin to get WYSIWYG functionality.

## Installing Movable Type

To install Movable Type, you need to download the install file from the Movable Type Web site <http://www.movabletype.org/>. Once you have done this, extract the Movable Type files and move them to your server. In your cgi-bin, create a folder called "mt." Next, move the mt-static folder to the main Web server directory. Then move the rest of the Movable Type files to the "mt" folder you created in the cgi-bin directory. Once you have done this go to <http://your.server.address/cgi-bin/mt/mt.cgi> to start the setup process.

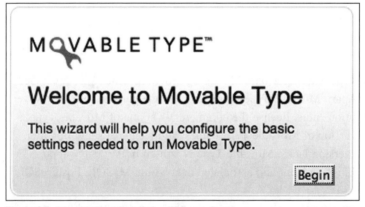

**Figure 9-1:** Movable Type Installation Welcome Screen

Movable Type requires several pieces of software to function correctly. The first thing the Movable Type setup does is check to see if you have all the necessary software. If all the necessary software is present, you will see the following screen:

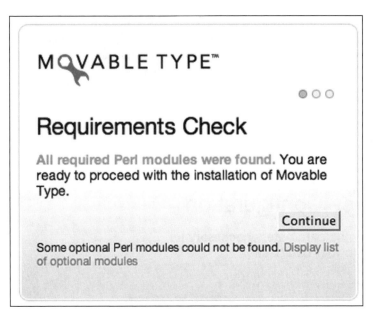

**Figure 9-2:** Movable Type Requirements Check

If the necessary software (Perl modules) is not present, you will be informed and asked to install the necessary software.

Movable Type does require a database to function properly, but you can use a MySQL, PostgreSQL, or SQLite database to store your data. If you are using MySQL to store your data you will be asked to input information about your MySQL database, including database name, username, and password.

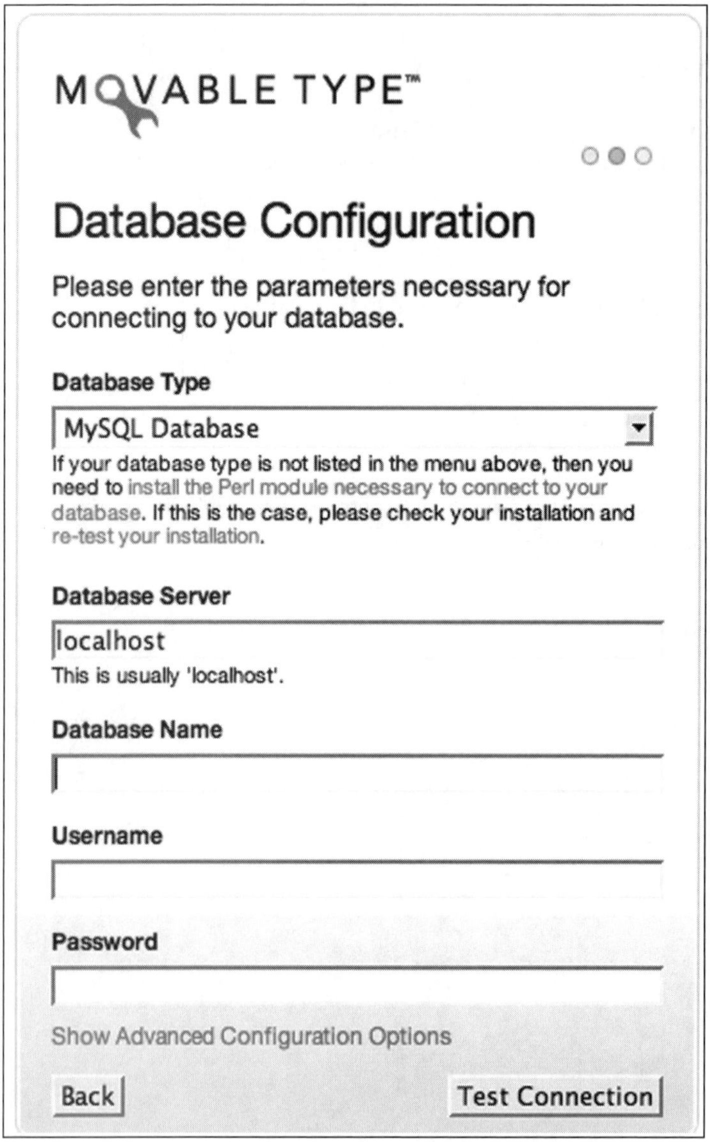

# MOVABLE TYPE™

○ ● ○

# Database Configuration

Please enter the parameters necessary for connecting to your database.

**Database Type**

| MySQL Database ▾ |

If your database type is not listed in the menu above, then you need to install the Perl module necessary to connect to your database. If this is the case, please check your installation and re-test your installation.

**Database Server**

localhost

This is usually 'localhost'.

**Database Name**

**Username**

**Password**

Show Advanced Configuration Options

| Back | Test Connection |

**Figure 9-3:** Movable Type Database Configuration

You need to set up a database and user in MySQL for Movable Type to use before you proceed through this section of the configuration. To set up the database and user in MySQL, first login to MySQL as the root user (mysql -u root -p). Next, create a database for Movable Type to use: (create database_name;). Last, create a MySQL user for Movable Type to use and give it the appropriate permissions on the

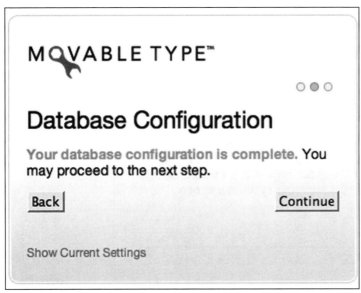

**Figure 9-4:** Movable Type Database Configuration OK

newly created Movable Type database, (GRANT ALL on database_name.* to user-name identified by 'password';). Make sure you write down the name of the database, the username, and password because this is the information you need to input into the database configuration screen. Once you have successfully done this you will see the following screen.

Next Movable Type will ask you to set up a mail server. There are two options: sendmail or SMTP Server. Unless you know sendmail is installed on your server, choose the SMTP Server option and input a valid SMTP server and e-mail address.

The last thing Movable Type will do is create a configuration file with all the information you have just input. This can be done two ways: either you can allow Movable Type to write the configuration to the server itself or you can copy the configuration information into a text file named >mt-config.cgi< and upload this file to the server. I recommend the second option because it is more secure and doesn't require you to change file permissions on the server. To do this click on the link labeled "Show the mt-config.cgi file generated by the wizard," and copy and paste the information in the text box into a text file. Save this as mt-config.cgi and upload it to the mt folder in the cgi-directory. Next check the box labeled, "I will create the mt-config.cgi file manually" and press Continue. You should see a message stating that you have successfully configured Movable Type.

Next, you will need to create your first user for Movable Type. This should be

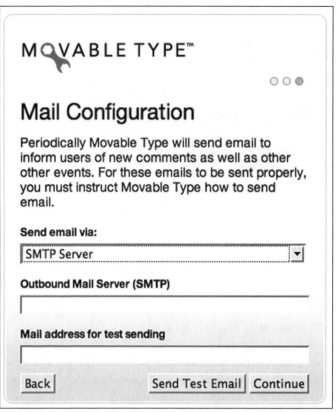

**Figure 9-5:** Movable Type E-mail Server Configuration

**Figure 9-6:** Movable Type Configuration Successful

your administrator account. Input a username, display name, e-mail address, password, and password recovery phrase.

You will be asked to create your first blog. Input the blog name, blog URL,

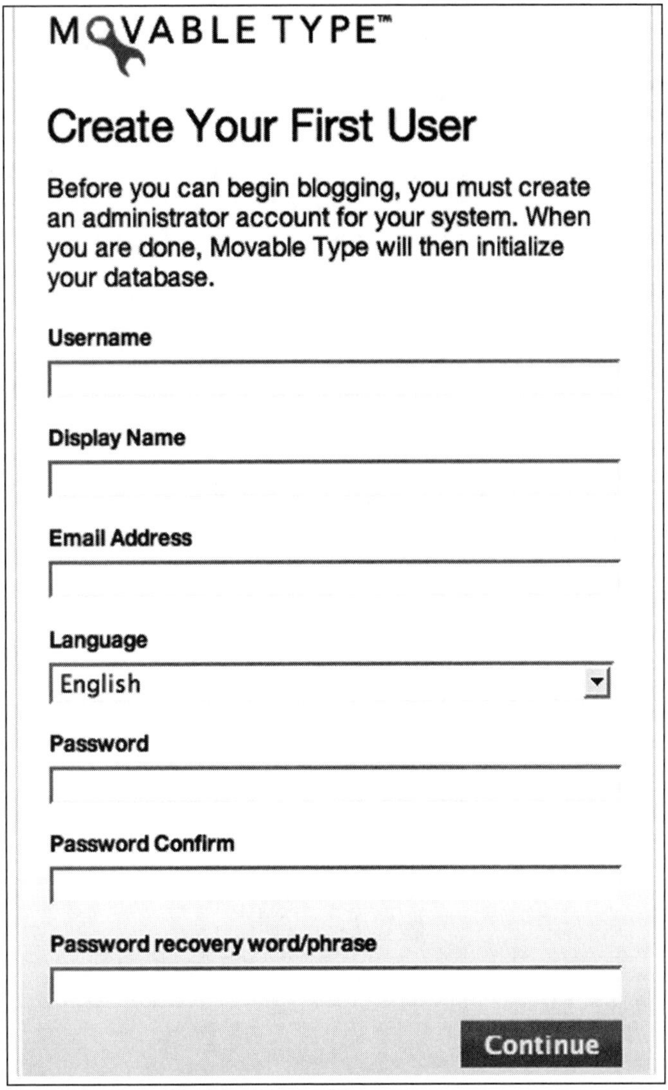

**MOVABLE TYPE™**

# Create Your First User

Before you can begin blogging, you must create an administrator account for your system. When you are done, Movable Type will then initialize your database.

**Username**

**Display Name**

**Email Address**

**Language**

| English | ▾ |

**Password**

**Password Confirm**

**Password recovery word/phrase**

Continue

**Figure 9-7:** Create First Movable Type User

publishing path, and time zone. Remember that your publishing path must be a directory to which the Web server has write access.

If you are successful, you will see the following screen which asks you to login.

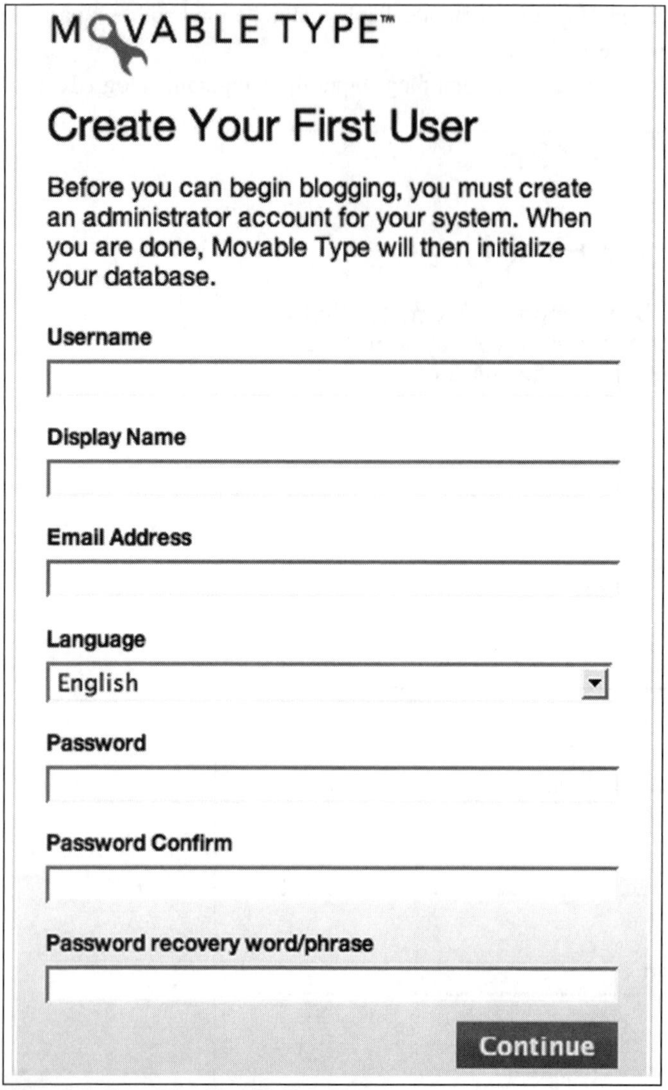

# MOVABLE TYPE™

# Create Your First User

Before you can begin blogging, you must create an administrator account for your system. When you are done, Movable Type will then initialize your database.

**Username**

**Display Name**

**Email Address**

**Language**

English

**Password**

**Password Confirm**

**Password recovery word/phrase**

Continue

**Figure 9-8:** Create First Movable Type Blog

**Figure 9-9:** Movable Type Installation Successful

# Blogging Basics

Once you have successfully installed Movable Type you will be able to start post-ing to your blog. You can do this using the Write Entry link. Creating a post in Movable Type is extremely easy. Text can be formatted using Microsoft Word-like buttons. Additionally, you can add images to your post.

Posts can also have tags, keywords, or categories added to them. One use-ful feature of Movable Type is the fact that you can schedule when a post is released to the world. This is nice if you want posts to come out at a specific time or pre-write content for your blog. You can also select whether or not a post accepts comments or trackbacks.

In addition to posts, version 4 of Movable Type allows users to easily cre-ate pages.

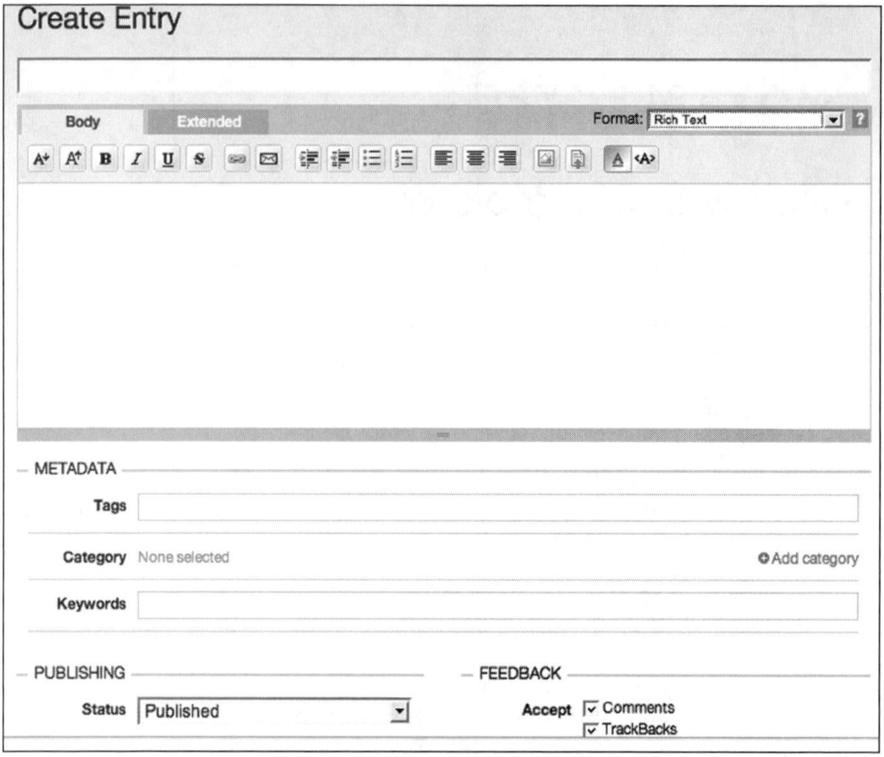

**Figure 9-10:** Movable Type Create Entry

## Customizing the Look and Feel

In early versions of Movable Type customizing the look and feel of a blog was an extremely convoluted process that required knowledge of HTML, CSS, and Movable Type templating tags. In Movable Type 4, developers have attempted to simplify this process by providing users with the styles and widgets. Both of these tools are Movable Type's response to the theme and widget features of WordPress.

Styles allow you to select a basic look and feel for your blog. To choose a Style, select Design and then Styles. From the Styles screen, you can browse the Default Styles, and the MT 4 Style Library to select a style for your blog.

Once you choose a style, you need to select a layout of that style and apply the design. If you are publishing your blog statically, applying the design won't change the look and feel of your blog. First, you need to republish your blog; the style manager provides a link for doing this.

If you don't like the styles provided as part of the default Movable Type installation you have several options. First, you can look for more style libraries and add them to your instance of Movable Type. To add another style library click the plus sign and input the URL for the style library. One repository for styles that is good is The Style Archive <http://www.thestylearchive.com/browse/>.

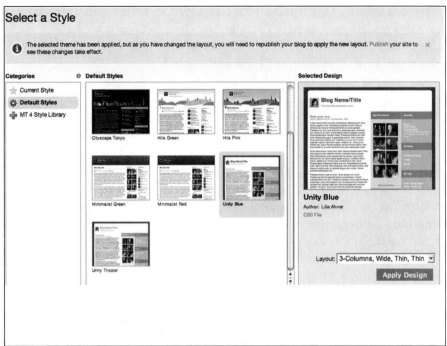

**Figure 9-11:** Movable Type Select a Style

**Figure 9-12:** Movable Type Republish Blog

Second, you can import a style from another source. Download the style, which will typically be a zipped file. Extract the style, so that a folder is created. Place this folder in the `mt-static/themes` folder on your Web server. Then you can select this particular style using the style manager. Lastly, you can build your own styles. This process requires knowledge of HTML and CSS and shouldn't be undertaken lightly.

Widgets allow users to arrange and manage content on a page just by dragging and dropping it. Unlike widgets in WordPress that can only be added to the blog's sidebar, widgets in Movable Type can be added to any piece of the page. The downside with this is that to insert a set of widgets you need to insert the widget code into the relevant Movable Type template. Some widgets that are readily available in Movable Type include: Calendar, Category List, Creative Commons License, Monthly Archive List or Dropdown, Recent Comments, Recent Posts, Search Form, Subscribe to Feed, Tag Cloud, and Technorati Search.

To take the best advantage of Movable Type templates, styles, and widgets, the default templates need to be rewritten to use modules. The advantage of modules is that they compartmentalize code so that it can be reused and easily updated. You can make modules for entries, the blog sidebar, the blog header, and the blog footer.

# Pointers for Posting

Movable Type includes a very simple and easy-to-use WYSIWYG editor for creating blog posts. With the editor, you can easily create and format text. The editor has buttons for making lists, adding links, centering text, and adding images. One of the nice things about Movable Type 4 is that it comes with a built-in asset management tool that you can use to keep track of your images, audio, and video. You can upload media as you are writing a post or ahead of time using the Create tab and Upload File link.

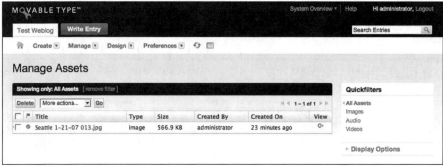

**Figure 9-13:** Movable Type Asset Management

As a result, adding images in Movable Type is a little different from adding them in other blogging platforms. By default, Movable Type allows you only to add images that you have uploaded to the Movable Type server. When you click on the image button you are asked to choose an existing image or upload a new one.

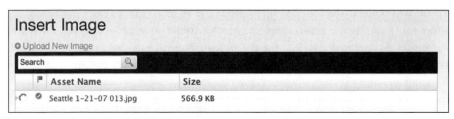

**Figure 9-14:** Movable Type Add New Image

Choosing an existing images is as simple as selecting it from a list. Uploading an image is slightly complicated. First, click the Upload New Image link. Then use the Browse button to find the image you want to upload on your local computer. Remember to size your image appropriately before uploading it, otherwise it won't fit properly into your post. Lastly, tell Movable Type where to upload the image. To keep all the images on your blog in a specific folder, we recommend you select the path, `Site Root/images`.

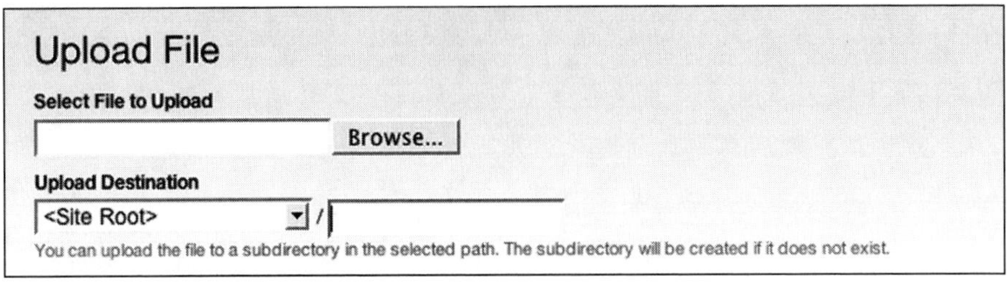

## Upload File

**Select File to Upload**

[                                    ] [ Browse... ]

**Upload Destination**

[ <Site Root>        ▼ ] / [                        ]

You can upload the file to a subdirectory in the selected path. The subdirectory will be created if it does not exist.

**Figure 9-15:** Movable Type Upload Image

Next, you will be asked for some information about the image: name, description, tags, and how you want the image aligned. Input this information and click on Finished.

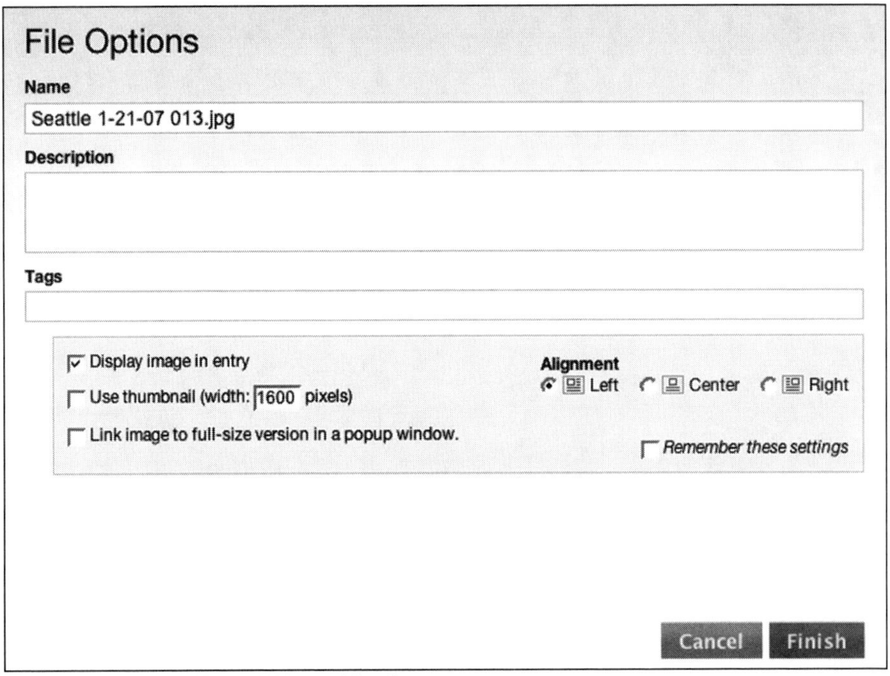

## File Options

**Name**

[ Seattle 1-21-07 013.jpg                                              ]

**Description**

[                                                                      ]

**Tags**

[                                                                      ]

☑ Display image in entry

☐ Use thumbnail (width: [1600] pixels)

☐ Link image to full-size version in a popup window.

**Alignment**

◉ ▣ Left    ○ ▣ Center    ○ ▣ Right

☐ Remember these settings

[ Cancel ] [ Finish ]

**Figure 9-16:** Movable Type Add Image Metadata

This will add the image to your entry.

Adding audio and video to Movable Type works similarly. Simply use the Insert File button to add the audio or video to your post or page.

# CHAPTER 10

# *Related Technologies*

## *Syndication*

Many different technologies are related to blogging. The most important of these is syndication. The basic idea of syndication is making content available to other sites and applications to use. This is accomplished by utilizing a form of XML for applications or sites to access via HTTP, the standards transmission protocol for the Web. Any application that is able to access the XML can access the syndicated content. Applications and sites that want to use the syndicated content are responsible for downloading the latest content via the XML transmission format. On the originating site, syndicated content is kept up-to-date and synchronized with the site's traditional content.

Syndication has many benefits both for the site where the content originates and the sites and applications that incorporate syndicated content. First, by syndicating content the originating site exposes its content to a wider audience by making it available across a number of different platforms. Second, syndication generates additional new traffic for the originating site. In contrast, sites that incorporate syndicated content are able to add information that has greater depth and immediacy to their pages. Additionally, by incorporating syndicated content, sites can create a more unified experience for their users. Examples of this include Web portals like NetVibes PageFlakes, and even Google's personalized home page.

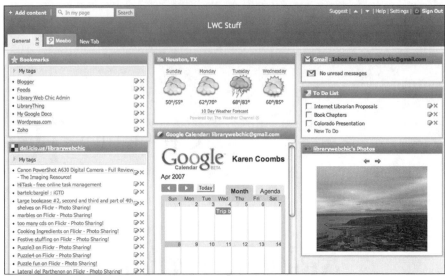

**Figure 10-1:** Example of Customized Netvibes Home Page

While early syndication efforts were focused on text, current syndicated content can be text, images, audio, or video. Because of this, syndicated content can be consumed by many applications including those on the desktop. The best example of this is Apple's iTunes, a popular program for managing music and other types of media. In the spring of 2005, Apple announced they were adding the ability for users to subscribe to streams of syndicated audio known as podcasts and created a directory where users could search these streams of content as part of iTunes.

There are two main types of syndication: RSS and Atom.

# RSS

RSS can stand for many things including: RDF Site Summary, Rich Site Summary, or Really Simple Syndication. RSS originated as part of the My Netscape portal and was later adopted and modified by Userland. As a result, there are several different formats of RSS but primarily two different branches: the 1.0 branch and the 2.0 branch. On the most basic level, each branch is designed to do the same thing and the two branches are similar in form. Each RSS feed is made up of a channel with a title and description and several different items. Each item also has a title, description, and a link to the original content. It is possible to include subject information about a given item in an RSS feed using categories. This is not mandatory though, and not all bloggers use this feature.

However, there are significant differences between the RSS 1.0 and 2.0 branches. The RSS 1.0 branch uses RDF, or Resource Description Framework (a W3C metadata model), to describe items and was not originally designed to handle non-text content, even though there is an extension that allows you to add media. The RSS 2.0 branch is less complex than RSS 1.0 and allows media to be included in the feed. As a result, RSS 2.0 is more commonly used for syndicating content other than text.

Below is a sample RSS 2.0 feed.

Let's examine the parts of the RSS 2.0 feed one at a time.

- <?xml version="1.0" encoding="UTF-8"?>: This is the the XML Prolog. Every XML document must have one of these. It indicates the version of XML, 1.0, and the character encoding, UTF-8.

## Educating Your Users About Feeds

- Write a post about what feeds are, how they can be used, and why they are helpful and beneficial to library users.
- Make sure to include next to your feed graphic a "What is this" link to a page which explains what feeds are to users.
- Consider creating a subscribe page that details all the different ways to subscribe to your feeds and sites. Include options for people to subscribe using many of the popular feed reading tools, and how users can subscribe to a particular category of posts if you use WordPress and categories.
- Hold a class for library users on news readers to educate them about how RSS and Atom feeds can be useful, and time saving.
- Use Feedburner to offer feed updates via e-mail for users who are unfamiliar or uncomfortable with news aggregators.
- Offer feeds of other relevant information for library users such as new materials, holds and pickups from the catalog, table of contents from journals, and customized searches of the catalog or library databases.

```
<?xml version="1.0" encoding="UTF-8"?>
<rss version="2.0"
       xmlns:content="http://purl.org/rss/1.0/modules/con-
tent/"
       xmlns:wfw="http://wellformedweb.org/CommentAPI/"
       xmlns:dc="http://purl.org/dc/elements/1.1/"
       >
<channel>
       <title>Library Web Chic</title>
       <link>http://www.librarywebchic.net/wordpress</link>
       <description>Resources for librarians who are inter-
ested in the application of web design and technologies in
libraries</description>
       <pubDate>Wed, 28 Mar 2007 15:34:17 +0000</pubDate>
       <generator>http://wordpress.org/?v=2.0.9</generator>
       <language>en</language>
              <item>
              <title>Reflections on Five Weeks to a Social
Library</title>
              <link>http://www.librarywebchic.net/word-
press/2007/03/25/reflections-on-five-weeks-to-a-social-
library/</link>
              <comments>http://www.librarywebchic.net/word-
press/2007/03/25/reflections-on-five-weeks-to-a-social-
library/#comments</comments>
```

**Figure 10-2:** Example RSS Feed

```
          <pubDate>Sun, 25 Mar 2007 19:25:43
+0000</pubDate>
          <category>General Thoughts</category>
<category>5+Weeks+to+a+Social+Library</category><category>onlin
e+education</category>
          <guid isPermaLink="false">http://www.librarywe-
bchic.net/wordpress/2007/03/25/reflections-on-five-weeks-to-a-
social-library/</guid>
          <description><![CDATA[ While of my other 5 Weeks
organizers have posted their own reflections on the 5 Weeks
experience and since I&#8217;m a little late to the game I
won&#8217;t reiterate what they have said already. Instead
I&#8217;d like to talk a little bit of what I got out of 5
Weeks.
When I got involved in [...]]]></description>
          </item>
          <item>
          <title>Airport Express as a Print Server</title>
          <link>http://www.librarywebchic.net/word-
press/2007/03/25/airport-express-as-a-print-server/</link>
          <comments>http://www.librarywebchic.net/word-
press/2007/03/25/airport-express-as-a-print-
server/#comments</comments>
          <pubDate>Sun, 25 Mar 2007 18:59:30
+0000</pubDate>
          <dc:creator>Karen</dc:creator>

          <category>General Thoughts</category>
<category>Airport+Express</category><category>printing</catego-
ry>
          <guid isPermaLink="false">http://www.librarywe-
bchic.net/wordpress/2007/03/25/airport-express-as-a-print-serv-
er/</guid>
          <description><![CDATA[ At my house my husband
and I have the great divide. I&#8217;m a Mac user. He uses
PCs. Unfortunately we have one lovely HP laserjet printer that
we want to share. This poses a problem for two reasons. One my
husband&#8217;s computer and the printer are downstairs. Since
he doesn&#8217;t leave his computer on [...]]]></description>
          <content:encoded><![CDATA[<p> At my house
my husband and I have the great divide. I&#8217;m a Mac user.
He uses PCs. Unfortunately we have one lovely HP laserjet
printer that we want to share. This poses a problem for two
reasons. One my husband&#8217;s computer and the printer are
downstairs. Since he doesn&#8217;t leave his computer on all
the time, this is a major pain in the butt. Second, if I try
to print through my husband&#8217;s PC the result is a gob-
bledygook page. Apparently the driver doesn&#8217;t work cor-
rectly on a Windows shared printer.</p>
```

**Figure 10-2:** Example RSS Feed continued

```
<p>I&#8217;ve been dealing with this for some time now, more
than three years in fact. However, since I started writing the
book and proofing drafts, it has become somewhat more problem-
atic. So I decided enough is enough and that I was going to
purchase a print server to allow us both to use the printer
over the network regardless of which computer we were on or if
another computer was on.</p>
<p>When I started looking at print servers I thought that this
would be a very simple matter. However, I hit a major obstacle
almost immediately. Most printer servers are wired printers
servers. Meaning you plug them into your router then you plug
the printer into the printer server. My problem was that my
router was in a different room and on a different floor from my
printers. So what I needed really was a wireless printer server
capable of connecting to my existing wireless router and that
my PCs and Macs could both connect to. After much searching I
realized that my best option was likely to use an <a
href="http://www.apple.com/airportexpress/">Airport
Express</a>.</p>
<p>Normally most people use their Airport Express while they
travel or to connect their stereo to iTunes remotely or as a
wireless router for their home network. Since I already have a
wireless router I really wanted just to have the Airport
Express to connect to my existing wireless network and allow
the computers on the network to send jobs to the printer. While
the documentation said this was possible and should be easy, I
was concerned that it might not work for two reasons.</p>
<ol>
<li>I have my wireless networking protected with
encryption</li>
<li>I use an access control list to limit what computers can
connect to my wireless network</li>
</ol>
<p>I was concerned that these two things would keep the Airport
Express from being able to get on the network. However, while I
did need to deal with these issues the solutions to these issues
were rather simple. First, I followed the instructions that came
with the Airport Express on configuring it. During this process
I was asked if I wanted to connect the Airport to an existing
network and what the encryption key was for that network. Next,
the MAC address for the Airport Express is on the physical
device. So all I needed to do was add this to my wireless
routers access control list. Adding the newly networked printer
to my Mac via <a href="http://developer.apple.com/networking/bon-
jour/">Bonjour</a> was a snap. Getting it setup for my husband
was slightly more complicated. I installed <a href="http://devel-
oper.apple.com/networking/bonjour/download/">Bonjour for
Windows</a> and was able to browse, see the printer, then add
it.</p>
```

**Figure 10-2:** Example RSS Feed continued

```
<p>Overall this setup took me less than a half an hour, which
was much less time than I anticipated and a fantastic result
by my standards. I&#8217;m even considering getting another
Airport Express to hook up my color photo printer in another
room.
</p>
]]></content:encoded>
                          <wfw:commentRss>http://www.librarywe-
bchic.net/wordpress/2007/03/25/airport-express-as-a-print-serv-
er/feed/</wfw:commentRss>
                  </item>
          </channel>
</rss>
```

**Figure 10-2:** Example RSS Feed continued

- <rss version="2.0"> ...</rss>: This is the root element of the RSS XML document. It contains all the other elements in the document. The version attribute indicates which version of RSS is being used, in this case version 2.0.

- <channel>...</channel>: This is the channel element and contains information about the feed itself. Actual items are not included in this section.

- <title>...</title>: When this element appears in the channel element, it represents the title of the feed or blog.

- <link>...</link>: When this element appears in the channel element, it represents the Web address of the page associated with the feed.

- <description>...</description>: When this element appears in the channel element, it contains a written description of the feed.

- <pubDate> ... </pubDate>: The last date on which the feed was published.

- <generator> ... </generator>: The application that created the feed. In this case, the WordPress blogging software.

- <language> ... </language>: The language in which the feed is presented.

- <item> ...</item>: This element is the container for all the information about a single item within a feed. In an RSS feed for a blog, an item is equivalent to a blog post.

- <title>...</title>: The title of the item.

- <link> ...</link>: The Web address of the item.

- <comments> ...</comments>: The URL of a page for comments relating to the item.

- <pubDate> ... </pubDate>: The date on which the item was published.

- <guid> ... </guid>: A string that uniquely identifies the item.

- <category> ... </category>: The category of an item. Category is a repeatable element, so an item can have multiple categories.

- <description>...</description>: A narrative description of the item. This is often a summary of the item. However, the description can also be the complete content of the item.

These are the basic elements of an RSS 2.0 feed. However, RSS 2.0 has the capability of being extended to include elements from other metadata schemes. The second item in the example RSS feed has this type of information added. To add other metadata schemes to an RSS 2.0 feed you need to define them as namespaces in the <rss> element. Below are the three additional namespaces that are defined in the example RSS feed.

- xmlns:content=http://purl.org/rss/1.0/modules/content/: This namespace allows you to include HTML encoded content into your RSS field

- xmlns:wfw=http://wellformedweb.org/CommentAPI/: This namespace is used for comments.

- xmlns:dc=http://purl.org/dc/elements/1.1/: This is the namespace for Dublin Core, a simple descriptive metadata scheme.

In the second item in the example RSS feed you will see the following additional elements from these namespaces.

- <dc:author>…</dc:author>: The author of the item.

- <wfw:commentRss> … </wfw:commentRss>: This element contains the URL of the RSS feed for comments on an item.

- <content:encode> … </content:encode>: The complete post including any HTML that the author may have inserted for formatting purposes.

# *Atom*

Atom is the Atom Protocol for Publishing. Developed to deal with a growing dissatisfaction with RSS, work on Atom began in 2003. There were several reasons for developing a new protocol for syndication. First, there are multiple incompatible and widely adopted versions of RSS. Atom was meant to be a standard, which could be implemented by everyone. Second, there was a need to develop a standard that was 100 percent vendor neutral. Third, since Harvard had copyrighted RSS and frozen the format, there was a need for a standard that was freely accessible by anybody. Last, there was a need for a standard that was able to easily handle different kinds of content. Atom meets all of these needs. As a result, the Internet Engineering Task Force adopted Atom in 2005.

Some blogging software such as Blogger use Atom as their primary method of syndication. However, since RSS has been around longer it is the more prevalent standard. Additionally, many proponents of RSS feel that Atom merely clouds the issue and makes it more difficult for applications to implement syndication and read syndicated content.

Below is a sample Atom 1.0 feed

```
<?xml version="1.0" encoding="UTF-8"?><feed
   xmlns="http://www.w3.org/2005/Atom"
   xmlns:thr="http://purl.org/syndication/thread/1.0"
   xml:lang="en"
   xml:base="http://www.librarywebchic.net/wordpress/wp-
atom.php">
   <id>http://www.librarywebchic.net/wordpress/wp-atom.php</id>
   <updated>2007-03-28T15:34:17Z</updated>
   <title type="text">Library Web Chic</title>
   <subtitle type="text">Resources for librarians who are inter-
ested in the application of web design and technologies in
libraries</subtitle>
   <link rel="self" type="application/atom+xml"
href="http://www.librarywebchic.net/wordpress/wp-atom.php" />
   <link rel="replies" type="application/atom+xml"
href="http://www.librarywebchic.net/wordpress/wp-
commentsatom.php" />
   <link href="http://www.librarywebchic.net/wordpress" />
   <rights type="text">Copyright 2007</rights>
   <generator uri="http://wordpress.org/"
version="2.1.2">WordPress</generator>
<entry>

<id>http://www.librarywebchic.net/wordpress/2007/03/25/reflec-
tions-on-five-weeks-to-a-social-library/</id>
     <title type="html"><![CDATA[Reflections on Five Weeks to a
Social Library]]></title>
     <updated>c</updated>
     <published>c</published>
     <author>
       <name>Karen</name>
       <email>librarywebchic@gmail.com</email>
       <uri>http://www.librarywebchic.net</uri>
     </author>
         <link rel="replies" type="application/atom+xml"
href="http://www.librarywebchic.net/wordpress/wp-
commentsatom.php?p=610" thr:count="0"   />
     <link href="http://www.librarywebchic.net/word-
press/2007/03/25/reflections-on-five-weeks-to-a-social-
library/" />
     <category scheme="http://www.librarywebchic.net/wordpress"
term="General Thoughts" />

     <summary type="html"><![CDATA[ While of my other 5 Weeks
organizers have posted their own reflections on the 5 Weeks expe-
rience and since I&#8217;m a little late to the game I
won&#8217;t reiterate what they have said already. Instead
I&#8217;d like to talk a little bit of what I got out of 5 Weeks.
```

**Figure 10-3:** Example Atom Feed

```
When I got involved in [...]]]></summary>
        <content type="html" xml:base="http://www.librarywe-
bchic.net/wordpress/2007/03/25/reflections-on-five-weeks-to-a-
social-library/"><![CDATA[<p> While of my other 5 Weeks organ-
izers have posted their own reflections on the 5 Weeks experi-
ence and since I&#8217;m a little late to the game I
won&#8217;t reiterate what they have said already. Instead
I&#8217;d like to talk a little bit of what I got out of 5
Weeks.</p>
<p>When I got involved in 5 Weeks to a Social Library I
thought that I would provide technical backbone support for the
project. Ironically, it didn&#8217;t work out that way. While
it was my intention to be more involved in getting Drupal set
up and running, my time disappeared into the morass of proj-
ects at work. Most of the time I ended up making suggestions
but not really doing much backend stuff.</p>
<p>Instead 5 Weeks led me down the road of screencasting, pod-
casting, and digital video. While these topics have been inter-
est to me for a while, I hadn&#8217;t yet had a reason to
explore them in any depth. 5 Weeks provided that opportunity
and challenge.</p>
<p>What I&#8217;ve learned about digital content will definite-
ly help UH Libraries in the future. We are just beginning our
own forays into screencasting and learning painfully how to do
it effectively. The software you use DOES matter and you need
to choose carefully based on your needs. While I like <a
href="http://www.techsmith.com/camtasia.asp">Camtasia</a> a
great deal, I believe it is overkill for simpler screencasts
in which are primarily browser or other application screencap-
ture. For these <a href="http://www.adobe.com/products/capti-
vate/">Captivate</a> is likely a better choice. However, if you
want to combine and blend different forms of media (Powerpoint,
video, screencapture, audio voice over, etc) then Camtasia is a
great piece of software because it allows you to lay tracks
like a traditional editing program. Final file size versus
quality was also an issue that we struggled with and ultimate-
ly I think to serve the needs of users best we may need to
provide them with several options (streamed, different sizes,
resolutions).<br />
The experience also made me think a great deal about the preserva-
tion of digital objects. What happens to all our 5 Weeks content
if Blip.tv disappears? Where will screencasts, podcasts and videos
that libraries create be archived for the future? I&#8217;m grate-
ful to the <a href="http://www.archive.org/index.php">Internet
Archive</a> for providing people with space. However, I think that
libraries need to take a larger role in providing space for pre-
serving this kind of content. Not just what they are creating in-
house, but what faculty, staff, and students are creating as well.
If we don&#8217;t live up to this obligation much will be
lost.</p>
```

**Figure 10-3:** Example Atom Feed continued

```
<p>More than anything else, Five Weeks taught me want a hum-
bling experience it can be to work with passionate, smart, and
dedicated people. My co-organizers constantly amazed me and
made me feel like I could be doing so much more. At the same
time, the participants interest and enthusiasm was a blast. It
is rare for me to come away from a conference session knowing
for sure that it was worthwhile for those adding. With Five
Weeks I never had those doubts and that is very
gratifying.</p>
<p>As to whether or not I&#8217;d be willing to do something
like this again, yes and no. Putting together and putting on 5
Weeks to a Social Library was an exhausting experience. The
weeks of the course itself ended up coming at a really bad
time in my life this year and if there is a next time I will
have to do a better job of scheduling so I don&#8217;t feel
like I&#8217;m losing my mind. The whole production and medium
intrigue and excite me greatly though. So it is likely you
will see my name attached to similar endeavors in the future
if only because I haven&#8217;t quite completely scratched the
running free online education and programming itch yet.</p>
]]></content>
    </entry>
    <entry>
    <id>http://www.librarywebchic.net/wordpress/2007/03/25/air-
port-express-as-a-print-server/</id>
    <title type="html"><![CDATA[Airport Express as a Print
Server]]></title>
    <updated>c</updated>
    <published>c</published>
    <author>
      <name>Karen</name>
      <email>librarywebchic@gmail.com</email>
      <uri>http://www.librarywebchic.net</uri>
    </author>
        <link rel="replies" type="application/atom+xml"
href="http://www.librarywebchic.net/wordpress/wp-
commentsatom.php?p=611" thr:count="0"   />
    <link href="http://www.librarywebchic.net/word-
press/2007/03/25/airport-express-as-a-print-server/" />
    <category scheme="http://www.librarywebchic.net/wordpress"
term="General Thoughts" />
    <category scheme="http://www.librarywebchic.net/wordpress"
term="Mac" />

    <summary type="html"><![CDATA[ At my house my husband and
I have the great divide. I&#8217;m a Mac user. He uses PCs.
Unfortunately we have one lovely HP laserjet printer that we
want to share. This poses a problem for two reasons. One my
husband&#8217;s computer and the printer are downstairs. Since
he doesn&#8217;t leave his computer on [...]]]></summary>
```

**Figure 10-3:** Example Atom Feed continued

```
     <content type="html" xml:base="http://www.librarywe-
bchic.net/wordpress/2007/03/25/airport-express-as-a-print-serv-
er/"><![CDATA[<p> At my house my husband and I have the great
divide. I&#8217;m a Mac user. He uses PCs. Unfortunately we
have one lovely HP laserjet printer that we want to share.
This poses a problem for two reasons. One my husband&#8217;s
computer and the printer are downstairs. Since he doesn&#8217;t
leave his computer on all the time, this is a major pain in
the butt. Second, if I try to print through my husband&#8217;s
PC the result is a gobbledygook page. Apparently the driver
doesn&#8217;t work correctly on a Windows shared printer.</p>
<p>I&#8217;ve been dealing with this for some time now, more
than three years in fact. However, since I started writing the
book and proofing drafts, it has become somewhat more problem-
atic. So I decided enough is enough and that I was going to
purchase a print server to allow us both to use the printer
over the network regardless of which computer we were on or if
another computer was on.</p>
<p>When I started looking at print servers I thought that this
would be a very simple matter. However, I hit a major obstacle
almost immediately. Most printer servers are wired printers
servers. Meaning you plug them into your router then you plug
the printer into the printer server. My problem was that my
router was in a different room and on a different floor from
my printers. So what I needed really was a wireless printer
server capable of connecting to my existing wireless router and
that my PCs and Macs could both connect to. After much search-
ing I realized that my best option was likely to use an <a
href="http://www.apple.com/airportexpress/">Airport
Express</a>.</p>
<p>Normally most people use their Airport Express while they
travel or to connect their stereo to iTunes remotely or as a
wireless router for their home network. Since I already have a
wireless router I really wanted just to have the Airport
Express to connect to my existing wireless network and allow
the computers on the network to send jobs to the printer.
While the documentation said this was possible and should be
easy, I was concerned that it might not work for two rea-
sons.</p>
<ol>
<li>I have my wireless networking protected with
encryption</li>
<li>I use an access control list to limit what computers can
connect to my wireless network</li>
</ol>
<p>I was concerned that these two things would keep the
Airport Express from being able to get on the network.
However, while I did need to deal with these issues the solu-
tions to these issues were rather simple. First, I followed
the instructions that came with the Airport Express on config-
```

**Figure 10-3:** Example Atom Feed continued

```
uring it. During this process I was asked if I wanted to con-
nect the Airport to an existing network and what the encryp-
tion key was for that network. Next, the MAC address for the
Airport Express is on the physical device. So all I needed to
do was add this to my wireless routers access control list.
Adding the newly networked printer to my Mac via <a
href="http://developer.apple.com/networking/bonjour/">Bonjour</
a> was a snap. Getting it setup for my husband was slightly
more complicated. I installed <a
href="http://developer.apple.com/networking/bonjour/down-
load/">Bonjour for Windows</a> and was able to browse, see the
printer, then add it.</p>
<p>Overall this setup took me less than a half an hour, which
was much less time than I anticipated and a fantastic result
by my standards. I&#8217;m even considering getting another
Airport Express to hook up my color photo printer in another
room.</p>
]]></content>
    </entry>
</feed>
```

**Figure 10-3:** Example Atom Feed continued

Let's examine the different elements that make up the Atom feed.

- <?xml version="1.0" encoding="UTF-8"?>: This is the the XML Prolog. Every XML document must have one of these. It indicates the version of XML, 1.0, and the character encoding, UTF-8.

- <feed> ...</feed>: This is the root element of the Atom XML document. It contains all the other elements in the document.

- <id> ... </id>: This element identifies the feed using a universally unique and permanent ID. Often if you have your domain name, it is the URL of your blog.

- <updated> ...</updated>: The last time the feed was updated.

- <title type="text"> ... </title>: The title of the feed. The type attribute in this element identifies how the information within this field is encoded. In this case, it is plain text.

- <subtitle type="text"> ... </subtitle>: This is a human-readable description or subtitle for the feed. The type attribute in this element identifies how the information within this field is encoded. In this case, it is plain text.

- <link rel="self" type="application/atom+xml" href="..." />: The Web address of the feed itself.

- <link rel="replies" type="application/atom+xml" href="..." />: The Web address for the comments feed for the page associated with the feed.

- <link href="..." />: The Web address of the page associated with the feed

- <rights type="text"> ... </rights>: Information about the rights related to this content.

- <generator uri="..." version="..."> ... </generator>: The application that created the feed, in this case, the WordPress blogging software. This element also contains uri attribute that tells you where you can find information about the application that created the feed and a "version" attribute that tells you what version of the application created the feed.

- <entry> ... </entry>: This element is the container for all the information about a single entry within a feed. In an Atom feed for a blog, an entry is equivalent to a blog post.

- <id> ... </id>: A Web address that uniquely identifies the entry.

- <title type="html"> ... </title>: The title of the entry.

- <updated> ... </updated>: The last time this entry was updated.

- <published> ... </published>: The date that this entry was created.

- <author> ... </author>: This element is the container for all the information about the entry's author.

- <name> ... </name>: The author's name.

- <email> ... </email>: The author's e-mail.

- <uri> ... </uri>: The Web address for the author.

- <link rel="replies" type="application/atom+xml" href="... " thr:count="..." />: The Web address for the feed of comments about this entry. Additionally, this element can have a "thr:count" attribute that represents the number of comments that exist for this entry.

- <link href="..." />: The Web address for this entry.

- <category scheme="..." term="..." />: Information about the category of the entry. An entry can have multiple categories. The "scheme" attribute of this element provides a Web address for where the categorization scheme comes from. The "term" attribute contains the actual term being applied to the entry.

- <summary type="html" ...</summary>: A short summary, abstract, or excerpt of the entry. This element also has a "type" attribute that is set to "html" if the content of the entry contains HTML markup.

- <content type="html" xml:base="..."> ... </content>: The full content of the entry or a link to the full content. In this example, the full content is in this element. This element also has a "type" attribute that is set to "html" if the content of the entry contains HTML markup.

As with RSS, it is important to note that not all of the previously mentioned elements will appear in all feeds or versions and that additional elements may appear. This happens because each piece of blogging software generates its feeds in a slightly different way. As you can see from examining the structure of an Atom feed it is more complex than RSS 2.0 and provides a flexible architecture for creating feeds.

# Feedburner

Because of the differing specifications for feeds and a growing need for blog owners to keep track of the number of people subscribed to their blogs, a company
called Feedburner developed. Feedburner is a Web-based tool that allows you to create a single feed for your blog that anyone should be able to subscribe to, regardless
of the feed reader they are using. Feedburner feeds have several advantages. They
have simpler URLs. The traditional RSS feed for Library Web Chic is
<http://www.librarywebchic.net/wordpress/feed/rss2>. In contrast, the Feedburner
feed URL is <http://feeds.feedburner.com/LibraryWebChic>. Additionally,
Feedburner keeps track of the number of people subscribed to a feed. A final advantage of a Feedburner feed is that it can mix feeds from multiple sources including
Flickr, del.ico.us, and your blog.

The first step in using Feedburner is to go to <http://www.feedburner.com> and
set up an account. Once you have an account you need to configure your feed in
Feedburner. This is done by entering the URL for your blog's feed into Feedburner.

Next, you need to add your feed's title and edit the Feedburner address for
your feed. Once you've done this, you get to a page where you can customize your
feed further. To do this click on the Optimize tab.

**Figure 10-4:** Create New Feedburner Feed

**Figure 10-5:** Optimize Feedburner Feed

You will see a section here labeled "Services." In order to make your feed easier to read in browsers and facilitate potential subscribers previewing and subscribing to your feed, you want to configure the Browse Friendly option. Additionally, enabling Smart Feed will allow Feedburner to transform your feed into a format (RSS or Atom) most compatible for the application accessing it. Lastly, you need to go to your blogging software and replace your existing feed link with a link to the Feedburner feed. Some blogging software like WordPress have plugins that will help you do this.

Feedburner contains many other helpful tools. The Analyze tab helps you keep track of the number of people subscribed to your blogs. This tab also provides information about the feed with which readers are subscribed to your blog, and which posts on your blog attracted traffic to your blog. Feedburner can also be set up to collect more typical Web site traffic statistics like visitors, page views, referrals, searches, and outgoing links.

The Publicize tab helps you market your weblog by providing additional services such as e-mail subscriptions. All of these tools can help you monitor your blog and improve it over time.

**Figure 10-6:** Analyze Feedburner Feed Traffic

**Figure 10-7:** Publicize the Feedburner Feed

## Increasing Your Subscribers

- Use Feed2JS or another feed integration tool to add items from your blogs to your library home page
- Create a link from your library Web site to all of your blogs
- Use a recognizable and user-friendly graphic in an easy-to-find location on your site to allow people to subscribe to your feed
- Make sure your blog includes the proper HTML tags in the header so that browsers recognize your feed and offer people the option to subscribe
- Use Feedburner to create a Smart Feed that is reader-neutral and easy for users to subscribe to
- If you are creating podcasts, make sure to list them in appropriate podcast directories such as iTunes
- List your blogs on the Blogging Libraries Wiki and Library Success Wiki as examples for other librarians
- Integrate information from blogs into course management systems or class Web pages

# Feed Readers

One type of application that is designed to consume syndicated RSS and Atom feeds is a feed reader or aggregator. News information was one of the first types of content to be syndicated. This is because news changes often and users want regular updates of this content. Syndication is the perfect way to facilitate this functionality. As a result, applications were designed to download and aggregate several "news feeds" and present them to the user. The news aggregator application would keep track of which news items the user had read and, if desired, only show the unread items to the user. As time went on, these tools were used to subscribe to information other than news. As a result, their name has morphed slightly from news aggregator to feed reader or aggregator.

Feed reader applications can be desktop applications or Web-based software. Both types of software perform the same function, but there are slight differences between them. Because desktop applications are installed on a given computer, they can only be used from that computer. Popular desktop feed readers include NetNewsWire, NewsGator, and FeedDemon. With the release of Office 2007 for Windows and Office 2008 for OSX, Microsoft has introduced RSS reader functionality into Outlook™ and Entourage™.

In contrast, Web-based feed reader applications are logged into via the Internet and therefore can be used from any computer with an Internet connection. There are several different Web applications for feed reading as well. Bloglines, one early Web-based feed reader, is still one of the most frequently used readers. While Bloglines is extremely popular, there are other feed readers that have additional functionality. Rojo was one of the first feed readers to offer tagging of feeds and items. Other feed readers allow you share items or your feeds with other users.

Recently, Google has also entered into the feed reader marketplace with Google Reader™. Google Reader offers tagging of feeds and items. Additionally, it allows you to share items or feeds that you subscribe to with others. While Google Reader is still part of Google Labs and not a full-fledged service, it appears to be setting the standard for Web-based feed readers.

Another relatively recent development is the addition of aggregator functionality to Web browsers. Firefox, Safari, and Internet Explorer all include native support for feed reading. However, it should be noted that this functionality is extremely basic when compared to full-fledged feed reader applications like Bloglines. Additionally, browser-based aggregators like desktop aggregators can only be used from the computer on which the browser is installed.

# Tagging

Tagging is the idea of marking up items with keywords that describe the object or relevance of that object to a given individual, a sort of personal metadata. Since individuals assign tags to an object, the tags are not part of a formally defined classification scheme. Additionally, tags are non-hierarchical and have no inherent architecture. This makes them highly dynamic and flexible in nature. Tagging originated in sites where users were allowed to categorize their own objects. In particular, the bookmarking site del.cio.us and the photo-sharing site Flickr pioneered tagging. Both of these sites allowed users to assign keywords to objects that they had uploaded to their account in the site. Over time, this idea of allowing users to add their own descriptive information to objects has migrated to other Web sites and applications. Many applications now allow users to add their own descriptive information about an object regardless of whether or not the user created, uploaded, or owns the object. In fact, <www.Amazon.com> allows users to tag books on its site.

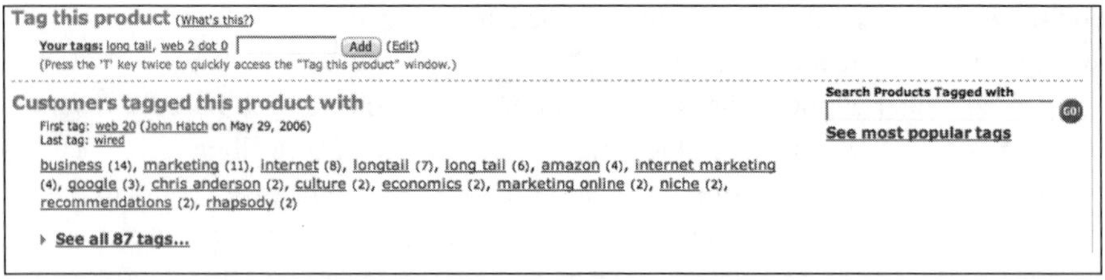

**Tag this product** (What's this?)

Your tags: long tail, web 2 dot 0 [        ] ( Add ) (Edit)
(Press the 'T' key twice to quickly access the "Tag this product" window.)

**Customers tagged this product with**

First tag: web 20 (John Hatch on May 29, 2006)
Last tag: wired

business (14), marketing (11), internet (8), longtail (7), long tail (6), amazon (4), internet marketing (4), google (3), chris anderson (2), culture (2), economics (2), marketing online (2), niche (2), recommendations (2), rhapsody (2)

▸ See all 87 tags...

**Search Products Tagged with**
[        ] (GO)
See most popular tags

**Figure 10-8:** Tagging at Amazon.com

As a result, of the growth of popularity of tagging, many blog posts now have tags assigned to them by the author or creator of that post.

As with most other forms of tagging, tags in blogs are typically used to describe the subject of a given post. On some blogs, tags are used synonymous with categories. However, on other blogs, categories and tags are used in different ways and provide different levels of subject granularity. Categories on blogs can be organized in a hierarchical fashion and as a result have a more defined structure than tags. Categories are much better suited to providing overarching subject divisions. In contrast, tags, because of their lack of structure, are better used to provide more detailed subjects of individual posts. Ultimately, how to use categories and tags is the choice of the blog owner(s).

One advantage that tags have is the ability to create a tag cloud. The idea of a tag cloud is to provide a visual representation of the subjects within a given set of objects. On a blog, this means providing a visual representation of the subjects included in that blog. Tag clouds are created so that subject terms that are used more frequently appear bigger and bolder in the cloud, while less frequent subjects appear smaller and fainter. Tag clouds can be extremely valuable in providing blog readers with a picture of the topics your blog covers.

**Figure 10-9:** Example of a Tag Cloud

A tag cloud is only one way of illustrating a folksonomy. Folksonomy is the name given to the free-form taxonomy that develops when informational objects are tagged. A folksonomy differs from a traditionally understood taxonomy in that there are typically no controlled vocabulary, no parent-child relationships, and both single and multiple terms available for use.

Many of the blogging software packages discussed in this book provide the ability to add tags to blog posts. In Movable Type, tagging is built in. The interface calls these "keywords" and you can add them to any post. To get the tags to display on your blog pages or as part of your feed you need to add code to your Movable Type templates. Creating a tag cloud in Movable Type is not simple. Instruction on how to do this is available on the Web at <http://www.saltpeppervinegar.co.uk/tutorials/adding_a_tag_cloud_to_movable_type_32.html>.

If you aren't familiar with the inner workings of Movable Type, this may prove difficult. As of version 3.2, tagging is also natively part of WordPress. Like Movable Type, you have to include tags in your template to include tags as part of your WordPress blog pages. In addition, you can also create a tag cloud to add to your blog's sidebar or on a separate page.

Tagging can provide your blog readers with better access to your blog's content by providing richer data to search and browse. Tag clouds can help readers see what topics you post most frequently and find related posts. For these reasons, tagging is a worthwhile addition to most library blogs.

## Mashups

Mashups are Web sites or applications that combine content from more than one source into a single user experience. As previously described, one significant advantage of syndicating content is that syndicated content is available for other sites and applications to use. Mashups take advantage of syndicated content by repurposing that content into a new application or site. Mashups can also gather content that is available from application programming interfaces (APIs). Additionally, mashups can use locally existing data as part of the experience.

Currently there are several different Web mashup applications that are capable of incorporating syndicated content. Many of these applications are designed to create portals for users. Two commonly used portal applications include Netvibes and Pageflakes. Search companies such as Google and Yahoo have also begun to develop mashup-driven portals.

Applications specifically designed for mashing up data from many different sets of data have recently appeared. Yahoo Pipes is the most well-known of these. Yahoo Pipes can take information from different syndicated feeds and Web services, bring it together, sort and filter it, and then produce output in a variety of formats from RSS to JSON. Another recent entry into this arena is Microsoft Popfly™, <http://www.popfly.com>, a combination portal and mashup site. At the time of publication, it isn't as popular as Pipes, but it has promise.

Syndicated content can also be incorporated into an existing Web site using Web scripting languages. The best solution to this problem for non-programmers is Feed2JS <http://feed2js.org/>. Feed2JS is a web-based tool that helps users create a Javascript that will incorporate an RSS or Atom feed into their existing site. According to the Web site, the process of creating a relevant Javascript is broken up into three simple steps.

1. "Find the feed source, the Web address for the feed.

2. Use our simple tool to build the JavaScript command that will display it.

3. Optionally style it up to look pretty."

Feed2JS allows users with little or no programming skills to easily incorporate an existing feed into their Web site. However, for those with more programming skills or desiring a non-Javascript-based solution, there are code examples in a vari-

**Figure 10-10:** Flickr and Blog Mashup

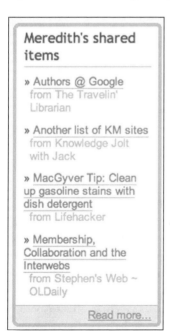

**Meredith's shared items**

» Authors @ Google
from The Travelin'
Librarian

» Another list of KM sites
from Knowledge Jolt
with Jack

» MacGyver Tip: Clean
up gasoline stains with
dish detergent
from Lifehacker

» Membership,
Collaboration and the
Interwebs
from Stephen's Web ~
OLDaily

Read more...

**Figure 10-11:** Google Reader and Blog Mashup

ety of programming languages available on the Web for how to do this.

While information from blogs can be incorporated into a mashup, a portion of a blog or an entire blog can be a mashup. There are many different kinds of content that can be incorporated into the mashed-up sections of blogs. One piece of content that is commonly mashed-up into a blog is photos from a photo-sharing site such as Flickr or Picasa.

This functionality has become so common that WordPress.com offers it as functionality of their software, and there are plugins for Movable Type and WordPress to do this. Other types of content that often get mashed-up as part of blogs include bookmarks from del.ico.us, shared items from Google Reader, and Google or Yahoo! Maps.

One example of a blog that is a mashup is Planet Code4Lib <http://planet.code4lib.org/>. Planet Code4Lib is an anthology, which combines posts from various members of the code4lib community and repurposes them into a new site with its own feed. While some may not see this as particularly earth-shattering, it is a good way to aggregate content, which a particular group might be interested in without a substantial amount of effort.

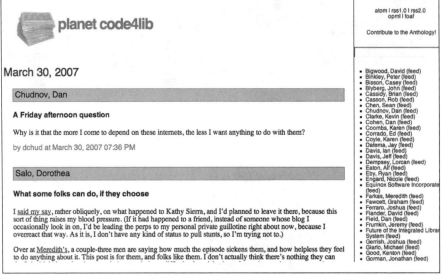

**Figure 10-12:** Planet Code4Lib Web Site

# Blogging Different Types of Media

While blogging originally began as a text-based medium, it has advanced to include other types of media including photos, audio, and video. Often this means that blog authors will include different types of media in a post. For example, if an author is discussing a video posted on YouTube, then he or she will likely embed a copy of that video at the beginning of the blog post. Many authors include photos or screen captures of items they are discussing in their blogs. However, some blogs are completely devoted to creating and sharing a particular type of media. Photoblogs, podcasts, and videoblogs are examples of this.

## Photoblogging

Photoblogging is creating a blog that is devoted to photos. Many professional and amateur photographers create photoblogs to display their work and get feedback for other photographers. Web applications such as Flickr have made photoblogging easy for the masses. Many different blogging software have plugins that allow you to add photos from Flickr to your blog posts. Users can also configure Flickr itself to post the photos to their blog by inputting the type of blog they have, their username and password, and the URL for their blog. In fact, Flickr allows you to configure more than one blog to which you can post Flickr photos. Once you have configured your blog(s) in Flickr, a Blog This button will appear next all your photos.

Photoblogging can have several applications for libraries. For example, libraries undergoing renovation or construction could set up a photoblog to document the process. Photoblogs also could be used for digitized collections of photos. Photoblogs could be used in conjunction with faculty for instruction purposes. Art faculty could work with librarians to set up a photoblog to display images relevant to their courses. Images relevant to the given week's lecture could be posted to a photoblog for students to look at and comment on.

## Podcasting

Podcasting is another way in which a blog can be devoted to a particular media. Podcasting is the distribution of audio files via a syndicated feed such as RSS or Atom. While many podcasts don't have a blog associated with them, some do. Having a blog and a podcast linked means that the blog can help promote upcoming "shows" and can provide a space for users to comment on content.

**Figure 10-13:** LITA Blog Podcasts

Like photoblogging, podcasting has many potential applications. Libraries can create shows about the library and distribute them. This could be especially helpful for user education. Libraries might consider creating a podcast for undergraduate students that begins with a basic introduction to the library and an audio tour, and then they can add progressively advanced material. For this to be successful, libraries will need to make sure that individual shows are released at times when the content will be of use to students.

Podcasts can also be used similarly to photoblogs to provide timed media content for a course. Librarians could work with music faculty to create podcasts of listening assignments. While this is similar to putting materials on reserves, podcasting takes library services to a new level by pushing content out to students.

Podcasting can also be an effective way in which to distribute conference content or information from an association. Recently, the Library and Information Technology Association piloted a project in which interviews with candidates for LITA offices were podcast. The hope of this endeavor was to better engage the LITA members in the election. These podcasts can be seen at <http://www.litablog.org/category/podcast>.

In the arena of podcasting conference presentations, the 2007 code4lib conference created audio files of all the sessions and put them up as a podcast after the conference. This move exposed the conference to a wider audience who might not have been able to attend in person.

## Videoblogging

Videoblogging is yet another type of blog devoted to a particular media, in this case video. Videoblogs are essentially blog posts of video. Like podcasts, videoblogs take advantage of the ability of RSS and Atom to distribute files. However, the files being distributed are video files, often MPEG-4 files, instead of audio files.

Videoblogs have several potential uses in a library setting. First, they can be used to distribute video content on a regular schedule to library users. The content that is distributed could be screencast tutorials about how to use the library, the weekly children's story hour, or a lecture series. In the academic environment, the library could work with professors to syndicate video of their weekly lectures for students. This would be especially helpful for distance-learning classes.

Second, videoblogs could be used to distribute content from library conferences. In 2007, the code4lib conference recorded all the conference presentations. Each of these videos could have been individually blogged and released as a videoblog. This idea could be extended upon by not only capturing video of presentations but also small interviews with participants.

As of yet there are few library video blogs or bloggers. One library videoblogger of note is David Lee King of the Topeka and Shawnee County Public Library. David's videoblog <http://davidleeking.com/etc/> is not necessarily devoted to library material. However, it will give you some ideas about how a videoblog works. Look at David's video on how his library is experimenting with a storefront "branch" in Second Life for an example of how videoblogging can be used for marketing purposes <http://davidleeking.com/etc/2007/03/second-life-at-work.html>.

# Creative Commons

Creative Commons is both a technology and a movement to allow individuals to easily mark their creative work with the freedoms they want it to carry. Creative Commons developed out of a need for a system that would allow people to legally share, reuse, and remix content. In Creative Commons, copyright owners can choose to grant some rights to other users up front rather than reserving all rights. The goal of Creative Commons as a technology is to make rights information readily available in three different formats: the Commons Deed, the Legal Code, and the metadata. The Commons Deed, which is in common language, allows users to know what they can do with an object. The Legal Code is the version meant for lawyers, and the metadata is readable by machines such as search engines.

There are several different types of rights that Creative Commons allows the copyright owner to grant or reserve. These rights include the right to share and distribute the content with others and the right to remix the content as part of another work. With Creative Commons, copyright owners can also designate whether or not someone using their work must attribute it. Additionally, copyright owners can specify whether or not the work can be used for commercial purposes. If you are already confused about which rights you might want to grant or keep, don't worry, the Creative Commons Web site <http://creativecommons.org> has a tool <http://creativecommons.org/license/> that will help you create the right kind of license for the rights you want to grant and keep.

Creative Commons licenses have grown so much in popularity that many sites for posting and sharing content on the Web have incorporated them. Flickr and Blip.tv, a site for sharing video and audio, both have options for a user to assign a Creative Commons license to an object they uploaded. Additionally, many bloggers employ Creative Commons for their blogs, and several blog software packages include the ability to create a Creative Commons license and add it to a blog. Movable Type includes the ability to assign a Creative Commons license to your blog and there is a Creative Commons license plugin for WordPress. Creative Commons is also important to blogs because it enables bloggers to more easily determine whether or not they can reuse content from another site as part of their blog.

CHAPTER 11

# *What is Possible with a Blog?*

L ibraries can use blogs for a number of different purposes from distributing news to acting as a surrogate for the catalog. How a library chooses to use blogs to better serve its users varies greatly from one library to another. Some libraries use blogs to communicate news to their users while other libraries use blogs for internal communication purposes. Blogs at some libraries serve as a way to distribute media such as audio or video to users, while at other libraries blogs serve as advertisements for services and events. Blogs at some libraries have even become the backbone of the library Web site and catalog. This variation in how libraries utilize blogs demonstrates the flexibility of blogs for creating content.

## *Blogs for News*

The classic way in which libraries use blogs is to distribute news to their users. This news can be concerning new materials, building projects, service interruption, or upcoming events. PaperCuts, Topeka and Shawnee County Public Library blog, <http://www.tscpl.org/papercuts> is a good example of a general library news blog. This blog has a variety of information about the library from news and events to reviews of books and videos.

# How to get people to read and revisit your blog

- Provide compelling content that draws users in by teaching them something, saving them time, or providing them with information they need to know.

- Make sure your blog is being updated regularly. Why would anyone read a blog that doesn't have new content for them?

- Consider creating blog content for specific user groups either via categories and tagging or by creating blogs for specific user groups such as teens.

- Allow users to comment and spark conversation between the library and users.

- Market your blog in print and via the Web. Get your blog's feed incorporated into the university or city Web site.

- Use media when appropriate to catch user's eyes and make for a more interactive experience.

**Figure 11-1:** Papercuts Topeka Shawnee Public Library Blog

Some libraries even develop blogs for specific users groups. At the Madison-Jefferson County Public Library, librarians and staff have developed blogs for their young adult <http://www.mjcpl.org/Library-Buzz/?c=Youth-Buzz> and children's user groups <http://www.mjcpl.org/Library-Buzz/?c=Kids-Buzz>. They integrate these blogs into portals specifically designed for these user groups. Using blogs this way allows the library to target the most relevant news to a specific user group.

**Madison-Jefferson County Public Library**

Your Library | Find Materials | Books-Film-Music | Local Heritage | Youth Pages | News & Events

kidszone

**Toolbox**

Search our Catalog...

Fiction

Kids Buzz

Kids events

Links

Our Collection

Staff Picks

Technology

Your Picks

**Contact Us**

Call children's librarian
Brenda Evans
at (812) 265-2744

**Kids Buzz**

**YOU WILL LOVE THIS BOOK!!**

I loved the Fonz when I was a kid. Now I'm all grown up and know that he is really an actor named Henry Winkler and I'm okay with that. I even think that Henry Winkler is a lovely actor and director. AND author.

Henry Winkler and Lin Oliver have written a wonderful series about The World's Greatest Underacheiver, Hank Zipzer.

Hank Zipzer is a fourth grader of the trouble making variety. However, it seems like trouble finds him more than he intentionally makes it. In the first book Niagra Falls or Does It, the teacher assigns a five paragraph essay about 'What I Did On My Summer Vacation'. What a nightmare!! Hank hates to write. He can't spell. He's highly allergic to lined paper. His brain is controlled by aliens...

Hank decides to be creative instead of writing an essay. Mayhem ensues. By the end Hank learns that maybe his brain isn't stupid, just wired a little differently. The reader learns that Hank is a character he/she wants to read more.

**Kids Events**

Friends of the Library Annual Booksale
Wednesday, Sep 26

**Click here to see all our events!**

**Booker says...**

Call our Dial-a-Story at (812) 265-2255 to listen to a funny and exciting tales.

**Figure 11-2:** Madison Jefferson County Public Library Kids Buzz Blog

One kind of event that might be well suited to a news-oriented blog is a library building project. Building projects cost millions of dollars and can be extremely disruptive to library users. Yet, library users are not often informed about such projects. A blog is a great way to keep the community in the loop about a building project. Georgia State University Library is doing this with its "Library Transformation News" blog <http://www.library.gsu.edu/news/index.asp?typeID=83>. The blog chronicles the renovation of two library buildings and provides updates to library users on the project's progress. In addition, to the main blog about the project, GSU also has created a photoblog <http://www.flickr.com/photos/gsulibrary/sets/> with images of the project using Flickr. In addition to keeping library users up-to-date on changes, this blog is a valued chronicle of the history of the library.

Another variation on the theme of using blogs for news is using them to provide readers advisory information or advertise new materials. Using blogs for reader's advisory purposes has several advantages. First, because blogs are simple and easy to use, readers advisory information can be more timely and current. Second, blogs afford the ability for multiple people to contribute. This can be invaluable if a library needs to spread the burden of creating content out across several staff members. Last, blogs are great for readers advisory because they provide a space for users to contribute comments. Comments about books from library users may be as valuable to other library users as the content created by library staff. There are several libraries that use blogs in this way including the Lansing (IL)

**Figure 11-3:** Georgia State University Photoblog

Public Library <http://lansinglibraryadult.blogspot.com/> and the library at
Colorado College <http://library.coloradocollege.edu/bookends/>. Each of these
blogs has its own interesting features. The Colorado College blog offers a way for
users to navigate by genre as well as links to the book in the catalog or
WorldCat.org. The Lansing Illinois Public Library blog features a way to search the
catalog as well as a way to instant message with a librarian.

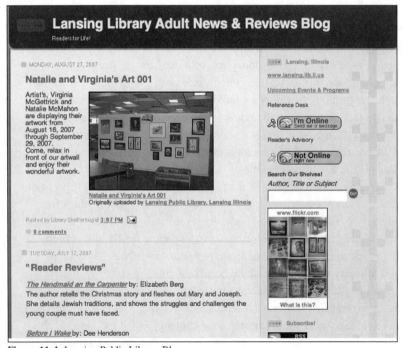

**Figure 11-4:** Lansing Public Library Blog

Blogs can also be used to promote new materials. Using a blog for this purpose has advantages over a simple text-based list. A blog can contain media such as book jackets to showcase materials and link back to the local catalog. A blog for new books can contain descriptions and/or reviews. A blog allows users to comment on new materials and provide feedback like, "Hey, there are not enough copies of this book." The Graphic Novels blog of the Regina Public Library (Canada) <http://www.reginalibrary.ca/blogs/index.php?blog=12 > uses the multimedia capabilities of blogs to advertise new graphic novels it has acquired. Notice the links back to the catalog, the summaries, and great book covers.

**Figure 11-5:** Regina Public Library New Materials Blog

Blogs can promote library events. Blogging events informs people about what is going on in the library. By placing events in a blog and categorizing them, libraries can allow users to subscribe to a particular type of event via an RSS feed. Darien Library (CT) has a blog for library events <http://www.darienlibrary.org/connections/events/>. One of the best features of this blog is the "This Week at the Library" post, which summarizes all the upcoming events at the library for a given week. This blog also highlights new materials being released.

**Figure 11-6:** Darien Library Events Blog

**Figure 11-7:** Homer Township Public Library Teen Events Blog

Libraries can promote events for a specific audience. The Homer Township Public Library in Illinois has done this with its Teen Events blog <http://www.homerlibrary.org/teenevents.asp>. This blogs features library-sponsored events that are of interest to teens. It also includes links to other information for teens and the library's contact information.

**Figure 11-8:** Business Blog at Ohio State University Library

Blogs can provide news and information to students and faculty in a particular discipline. These subject blogs are extremely popular and useful in academic libraries. One of the best examples of a subject blog is the Business Blog at Ohio State University <http://www.library.ohiou.edu/subjects/businessblog/>. This functions as a portal for business faculty and students by providing up-to-date news and information. It also contains contact information for the subject specialist.

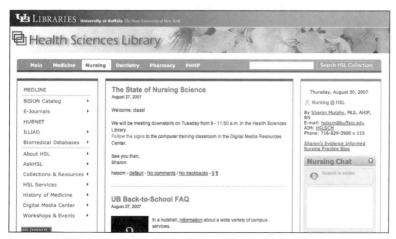

**Figure 11-9:** University of Buffalo Health Sciences Library Nursing Blog

The Nursing blog at the Health Sciences Library at the University at Buffalo (NY) <http://libweb.lib.buffalo.edu/hslblog/Nursing/> is another good example of a portal-like subject blog. This blog features news for nursing students; provides a Meebo chat widget for communication with a librarian, and links to relevant nursing resources.

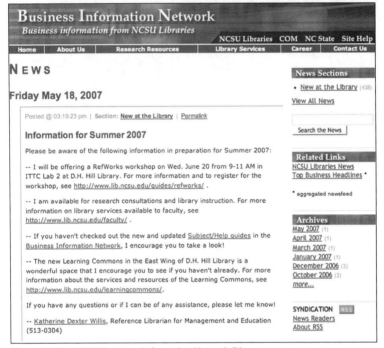

**Figure 11-10:** NCSU Business Information Network Blog

Another interesting subject blog is the Business Information Network at North Carolina State University <http://www.lib.ncsu.edu/news/business>. A blog for business faculty and students, this blog takes a slightly different approach than OSU's business blog by focusing more specifically on news and being less portal-like.

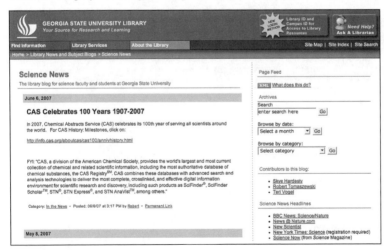

**Figure 11-11:** Georgia State University Library Science News Blog

Another academic library with a number of subject blogs is Georgia State University. GSU's subject blogs not only feature information about new library services, electronic journals, and reference titles, but they also provide links to other sources for news in a particular discipline.

The strength of subject blogs is that they allow subject librarians to target specific resources and tools to their faculty and students. Faculty and students are given a place where they can comment and converse with their subject specialist. Another strength of a subject blog is that users (via RSS) can keep current with the latest library news in their discipline without having to visit the library Web site regularly. This can be a huge benefit for faculty. However, most faculty are unaware of RSS and Atom and need to be educated on how this tool makes communication more efficient.

## Blogs for Internal Communication

In addition to using blogs to communicate with library users, several libraries are using blogs to facilitate internal communication. The University of Houston Libraries use blogs to facilitate communication among staff. Initially, blogs were used at UH Libraries to disseminate information about the Libraries Strategic Direction process and gather feedback from library staff as the directions were being developed. However, since that time blogs have become an important way for many groups within the Libraries to communicate. Staff and librarians who work the reference desk use the Academic Research Center (ARC) blog to distribute information about what is going on at the reference desk. This blogs often contains information about the reference questions students are asking, technical issues occurring with computers or printers, and other ongoing issues. To make sure that staff see the latest

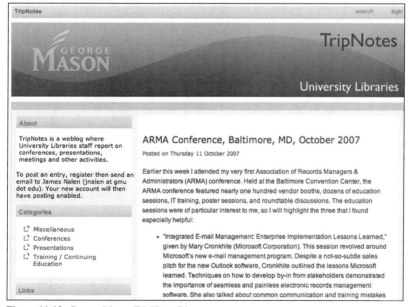

**Figure 11-12:** George Mason TripNotes Blog

information on the blog, the staff computers at the reference desk have the ARC blog as their Active Desktop. Additionally, the Libraries Instruction Team uses a blog to post the latest developments and news in the area of information literacy.

The University of Houston is just one organization using blogs to facilitate internal communication. Some libraries use blogs internally to distribute information about professional development. Both the Wake Forest Libraries and the library at George Mason University use weblogs in this way. George Mason TripNotes weblog <http://timesync.gmu.edu/tripnotes/> is used by library staff to distribute information about their professional development activities such as conferences, presentations, and meetings.

Wake Forest University Libraries professional development blog <http://blog.zsr.wfu.edu/pd> contains very similar kinds of information.  In both of these blogs, many of the posts are extremely detailed in nature. This level of detail is essential in order to summarize conference presentations and workshops for other library staff. One feature that sets the Wake Forest blog apart is its efficient use of categories to organize posts and direct readers to the most relevant information.

**Figure 11-13:** Wake Forest University Libraries Professional Development Blog

Blogs can also be used to gather feedback and document changes and decisions. The library for the Chicago-Ken College of Law at the Illinois Institute of Technology uses a blog to document its electronic resource trials and gather feedback on these trials. Via the blog, reference librarians can post their reviews or discoveries in the comments. One strength of using a blog this way is that the selection process and the feedback gathered as part of it is well documented to future collection development discussions. Similar to this is Kansas State University Libraries use of blogs to provide internal documentation to staff. Their SFX Documentation blog provides simple internal documentation about the SFX OpenURL resolver (SFX is the Ex Libris OpenURL product) updates, and enhancements for library staff.

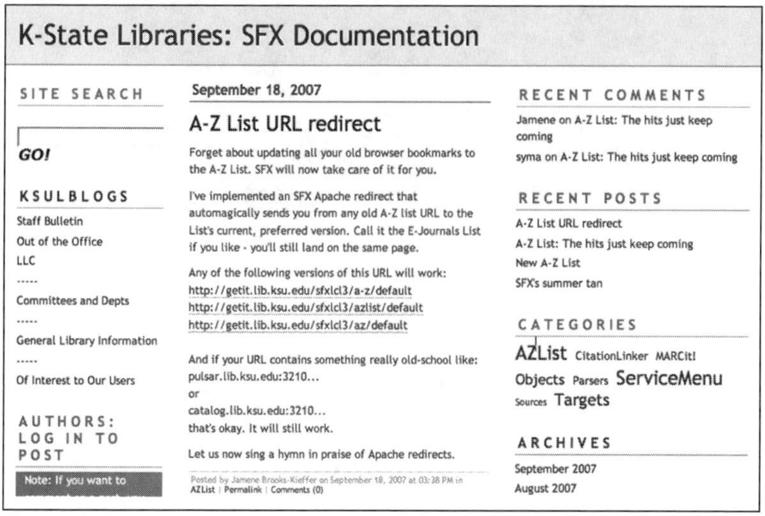
K-State Libraries: SFX Documentation
SITE SEARCH
GO!
KSULBLOGS
Staff Bulletin
Out of the Office
LLC
.....
Committees and Depts
.....
General Library Information
.....
Of Interest to Our Users
AUTHORS: LOG IN TO POST
Note: If you want to
September 18, 2007
A-Z List URL redirect
Forget about updating all your old browser bookmarks to the A-Z List. SFX will now take care of it for you.
I've implemented an SFX Apache redirect that automagically sends you from any old A-Z list URL to the List's current, preferred version. Call it the E-Journals List if you like - you'll still land on the same page.
Any of the following versions of this URL will work:
http://getit.lib.ksu.edu/sfxlcl3/a-z/default
http://getit.lib.ksu.edu/sfxlcl3/azlist/default
http://getit.lib.ksu.edu/sfxlcl3/az/default
And if your URL contains something really old-school like:
pulsar.lib.ksu.edu:3210...
or
catalog.lib.ksu.edu:3210...
that's okay. It will still work.
Let us now sing a hymn in praise of Apache redirects.
Posted by Jamene Brooks-Kieffer on September 18, 2007 at 03:38 PM in AZList | Permalink | Comments (0)
RECENT COMMENTS
Jamene on A-Z List: The hits just keep coming
syma on A-Z List: The hits just keep coming
RECENT POSTS
A-Z List URL redirect
A-Z List: The hits just keep coming
New A-Z List
SFX's summer tan
CATEGORIES
AZList CitationLinker MARCit!
Objects Parsers ServiceMenu
Sources Targets
ARCHIVES
September 2007
August 2007

**Figure 11-14:** Kansas State University Libraries SFX Documentation Blog

All of these examples demonstrate that blogs can be an extremely powerful tool for both distributing information and gathering feedback within an organization.

# *Organizational Blogs*

Several library organizations are also using blogs to communicate with their users. These blogs range from those of associations such as the Public Library Association to those of consortia such as the Michigan Library Consortia's MLC Blog.

Blogging has become an important activity for several divisions of the American Library Association. The Association of College and Research Libraries (ACRL), the Library and Information Technology Association (LITA), and the Public Library Association (PLA) all have distinctive and well-developed blogs. ACRLog <http://acrlblog.org/>, the blog of ACRL, has a small core group of writers including Steven Bell and Barbara Fister. This blog focuses on discussing issues in academic libraries rather than distributing news within the organization. Posts range in topics from free speech and academic freedom to information literacy.

In contrast, LITA Blog <http://www.litablog.org>, the blog of LITA, places greater focus on distributing information about the goings-on in the organization to its members. Information about upcoming events and volunteer opportunities are often posted to the blog. Moreover, one of the primary pieces of content of LITA Blog is posts from sessions at conferences such as LITA Forum, ALA Midwinter, and ALA Annual. Almost all of the conference posting is done by an extensive group of volunteer bloggers. This is one major difference between ACRLog and LITA Blog. While ACRLog has a small group of authors, LITA Blog has a huge group of authors that may only contribute one or two posts. In 2006-2007, LITA Blog created several podcasts of content for their readership including interviews with candidates for office with LITA and recordings of programs at the Midwinter and Annual meetings.

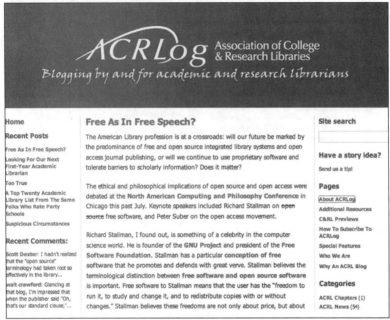

**Figure 11-15:** ACRLog

PLA Blog <http://plablog.org/> has content that is a mix of that on LITA Blog and ACRLog. PLA Blog promotes initiatives of the Public Libraries Association, provides press releases and announcements, discusses technology trends in public libraries, and encourages professional development of public librarians. Furthermore, PLA blog also contains blog posts, which are summaries of conference sessions. Like LITA Blog, posts at PLA blog come from a wide range of individuals.

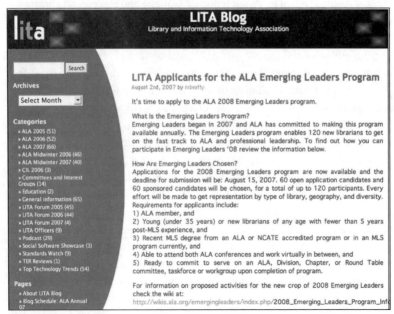

**Figure 11-16:** LITA Blog

**Figure 11-17:** PLA Blog

Blogs are also being used by local and regional consortias to distribute information to their members. The Michigan Library Consortium blog <http://www.mlcnet.org/blog/> provides members with news and information, highlights programming the consortia is offering, and provides information about trends in libraries.

**Figure 11-18:** Michigan Library Consortium Blog

The Wisconsin Library Association <http://wlaweb.blogspot.com/> is also using a blog to communicate with its members. The blog highlights news, upcoming events, and reports from conferences and provides information on library advocacy. The conference reports on this blog are excellent and use a good mix of text and photos to convey information to readers, as well as links to additional information related to the sessions.

**Figure 11-19:** Wisconsin Library Association Blog

The Boston Regional Library System's blog <http://blog.bpl.org/brls/> contains very similar content but seems to focus more on news, new services the system is offering, and important upcoming events. One great thing about this blog is that it actually is the home page for the consortia. Using a blog in this way allows the consortia to provide the most recent and relevant information to site visitors. To enable readers to easily move from news to other information they need within the consortia's Web site, this blog home page has links back to the rest of the consortia's Web pages in the sidebar navigation.

We've barely scratched the surface in this chapter in presenting what is possible with a blog. We suggest that if you want to see what other libraries are doing with blogs you visit the Blogging Libraries Wiki <http://www.blogwithoutalibrary.net/links/index.php?title=Welcome_to_the_Blogging_Libraries_Wiki>, and Library Blogs website <http://www.libdex.com/weblogs.html>.

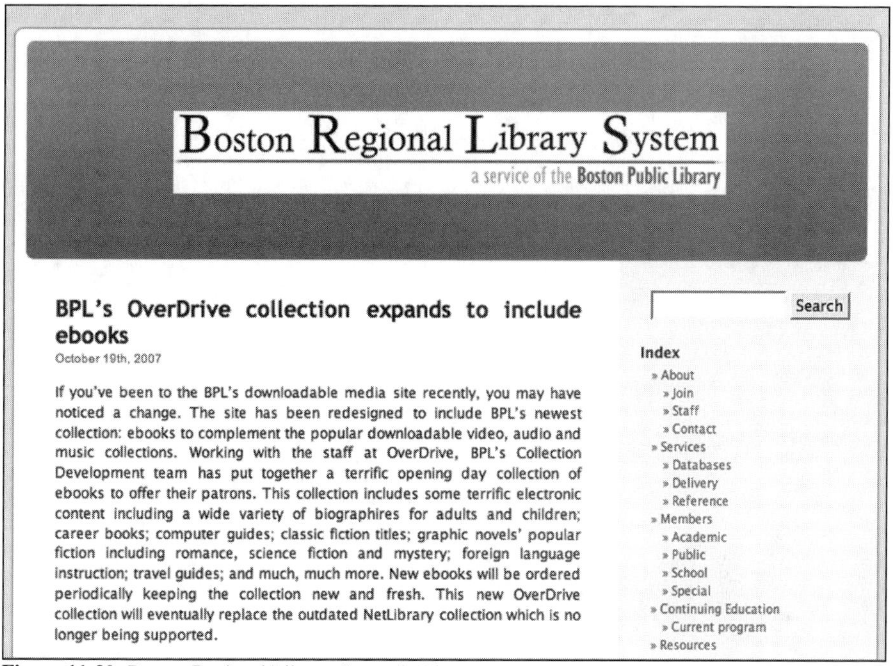

**Boston Regional Library System**
a service of the **Boston Public Library**

### BPL's OverDrive collection expands to include ebooks

October 19th, 2007

If you've been to the BPL's downloadable media site recently, you may have noticed a change. The site has been redesigned to include BPL's newest collection: ebooks to complement the popular downloadable video, audio and music collections. Working with the staff at OverDrive, BPL's Collection Development team has put together a terrific opening day collection of ebooks to offer their patrons. This collection includes some terrific electronic content including a wide variety of biographires for adults and children; career books; computer guides; classic fiction titles; graphic novels' popular fiction including romance, science fiction and mystery; foreign language instruction; travel guides; and much, much more. New ebooks will be ordered periodically keeping the collection new and fresh. This new OverDrive collection will eventually replace the outdated NetLibrary collection which is no longer being supported.

Search

Index
» About
    » Join
    » Staff
    » Contact
» Services
    » Databases
    » Delivery
    » Reference
» Members
    » Academic
    » Public
    » School
    » Special
» Continuing Education
    » Current program
» Resources

**Figure 11-20:** Boston Regional Library System's Blog

# CHAPTER 12

# *Blog Culture*

E very new form of communication has with it some cultural affectations that come to be norms. Blogs have been around long enough that they have their own language and shorthand, as well as standards and behaviors that mark you as a positive member of the blogosphere. Like many sets of online standards, these "rules" are flexible and nearly change constantly, but they make for a set of best practices for blogging that enhance the form for everyone.

In the same way that travel to a foreign country sometimes illustrates our own unconscious habits, blogs are slightly different than traditional Web sites. If you are new to blogging, read this chapter before you start posting and it may save you from being the stereotypical "bad American."

The first thing to have in mind when writing a blog post is that the best blogs have a voice, a point of view, a person behind the screen. While blogs are often referred to as a form of citizen journalism, if you write in a completely neutral journalistic tone, your posts will have a flatness to them that is difficult for people to consume. Especially for libraries using blogs as a marketing/advertising tool, pay attention to the tone you use and make sure that it accurately reflects the purposes of the blog. If you want to use the blog to draw patrons to the library, write with that in mind. If you are advertising your library, be excited about it!

It is very common for blogs to repost content that has been re-purposed from other Web sites or even other blogs. In fact, some of the most popular blogs in the world are nothing more than aggregators for content from elsewhere. This is true even in the library blogosphere, where memes travel from blog to blog over the course of days. If you repurpose content from another blog or pick up on a story that was originally mentioned somewhere else, you should credit the original source with a link back to its content.

Trackback through links is important, not only because it is part of responsible research to give credit to your sources but also because technologically most blogs "see" those incoming links and can therefore tell who and what is being said about the post in question. This is another piece in the conversation puzzle. But more importantly, links are the currency of the Web. In network theory, Metcalfe's Law says that the value of a system grows at approximately the square of the number of users of the system. That is, for any network, adding a node increases the value of that network. Adding a link to any piece of information on the Web increases the value of that piece of information from the perspective of search engines and increases its findability. Every bit of content that you re-purpose and link to becomes more valuable simply by the fact that you have chosen to do so. This could be seen as a new form of peer-review; not in the sense of validating the information but as a sort of interestingness measurement. Any information that has many links to it is, by definition, interesting to many people.

Anonymity has been a hot topic in the library blogosphere in 2007, and authorship is an issue that should be discussed early in the development of a library blog. There are many choices for libraries as far as the amount of information that is given about the identity of the person behind the blog, ranging from straightforward (the person blogs for the library but under his own name) to the more complex (different people blog under the same *nom de plume*, such as "The Reference Department"). For the purposes of a blog that represents your library, having names attached can only help personify the library for patrons and make them more comfortable interacting both virtually and directly with the library.

For any library blog that has minors as a patron base (school or public), there is another conversation to be had regarding comments on your blog. Comments are an intrinsic part of communication via a blog, but there are certainly limitations on the extent to which you may wish to allow comments, especially anonymous ones. You can mitigate potential abuse early on by moderating (reading and approving or disapproving) each comment as it comes through. As the blog grows in usage, however, moderation becomes more and more time-consuming. In the same way that you have a code of conduct for your physical library, it can help to have a written policy for comment moderation that you can point to if it becomes necessary.

A number of conventions regarding the appearance of a blog are somewhat separate from the structure of the information. Most blogs have a header of some sort that identifies it either via logo or text, and that header links back to the main page of the blog. Most blogs have a template that is organized roughly in columns, with the main column containing the posts from the blog and secondary or tertiary columns that contain other information. There is normally a footer on each page that contains meta-information about the blog and/or the author. Sticking with these layout conventions help reinforce the feel of your blog *qua* blog.

# Blog Code of Conduct

In March 2007, on his blog O'Reilly Radar <http://radar.oreilly.com/archives/2007/03/call_for_a_blog_1.html>, Tim O'Reilley suggested seven rules that would make up a Blog Code of Conduct:

---

1. Take responsibility not just for your own words, but for the comments you allow on your blog.

2. Label your tolerance level for abusive comments.

3. Consider eliminating anonymous comments.

4. Ignore the trolls.

5. Take the conversation offline, and talk directly, or find an intermediary who can do so.

6. If you know someone who is behaving badly, tell them so.

7. Don't say anything online that you wouldn't say in person.

---

We've already covered some of these. Rules 1 and 2 fall under the "control" discussion above, where libraries pay attention to the conversation and preemptively manage comments via policy. Let's take a closer look at the remaining rules and see how they might apply to library blogs.

Rule 3 as proposed by O'Reilly is potentially difficult for libraries. "Eliminating anonymous comments" conflicts somewhat with the library privacy standards for patron data. If a patron wants to comment on a book anonymously, there are good arguments for letting them. However, anonymity breeds a boldness of voice that is often absent if names are attached. This is an area where local decisions become important, and there needs to be a discussion between the librarians to see what the appropriate answer is for your specific library. There may be existing standards from which to draw. For instance, are there policies covering the use of a public bulletin board in your library where you allow patrons to post flyers? A blog isn't so different from a public posting space, and it is very likely that the same sorts of language can be used for both.

Rules 4 through 7 are good suggestions for online behavior, regardless of whether you are dealing with a blog or an e-mail listserv. They are just good virtual communication rules. If you aren't familiar with the term, a troll is someone who visits a location online for the purpose of argument or to cause trouble without contributing to the conversation positively. Someone who visits a library blog and says, "Libraries are stupid and stupid people work there," is a troll; that person is simply looking for an argument. Ignoring trolls is a good idea and will cause the stress level of dealing with the blog to go down.

In a situation where a discussion on the blog is getting heated, taking the conversation offline can moderate some of the emotion involved. This is largely to do with the distance inherent with virtual communication and the lack of context or tone to text. When an online conversation is moved offline, it is sometimes easier to get to the heart of the matter and clear up misunderstandings. Especially with patrons, there should always be the option to allow them to talk to an actual person in the library where disagreements are concerned.

Rule 7 could be expanded on to include "don't say anything online that you wouldn't say in person to everyone you know." With Google indexing and the Internet Archive scraping pages into its Wayback Machine, that thing you said can haunt you for a very long time. It will almost certainly be read by the one person you don't want; consider posting something to a blog to be the same as posting it publicly to the world and everyone in it. It is also a good idea to remind patrons of this fact when commenting.

All of these decisions, like many regarding appropriate content, are local ones. You should decide your comfort level and the comfort level of your community as you start blogging.

# *Community*

Blogs engender community by their nature. There are two pieces that make blogs particularly good at forming a community of users: their communicative nature and their connectivity. The library blogging community has grown so large that it is impossible to know or keep up with all of them, but it is very common to find a few blogs that are interesting and discover that they are linked to each other and communicate between one another. If you find good examples of, for instance, public librarians discussing reference services, those blogs will probably know about each other. These local communities exist for all sorts of blogs, from the public to the special interest.

Like moving into a new physical community, starting a blog on a specific subject is more comfortable the more familiar you are with the lay of the land. You should always read blogs and see what the conversations and personalities are like as you begin to set one up. What are other libraries doing? How are they handling specific issues? By reading the most popular blogs on a topic, you automatically get the benefit of seeing best practices in action. That blog wouldn't be popular if it wasn't doing something right, and you could do far worse than mimic some of their processes.

The technological connectivity behind blogs, things like trackback and RSS, allow for a level of automated interconnectivity that enhances the community aspects. Especially used by public and school libraries, but often ignored by academic libraries, is the ability to use your blog as a stage for presenting a variety of informational sources to your patrons. If you are a public library, what would be better for your patrons than becoming a destination for information about your area? Pulling in the RSS feeds of other community blogs enhances your own blog and makes it a more useful tool for your patrons.

# Being Native

In the world of blogs, being native just means respecting the pre-existing norms. This is especially true when you are commenting on a blog that is not your own or writing a post that draws from or is inspired by a post on another blog. Thanks to the magic of trackback, the owner of the blog you are discussing will see your comment as long as you link to them. People can follow the conversation across multiple blogs, and you should use Trackback to allow them to see the discussion as a courtesy to the person you are discussing. Consider it a form of citation, giving credit where credit is due.

There are other norms for your blog that are worth following, some of which are extensions of generic Web design norms. For instance, blogs almost universally follow a basic columnar layout for their template of either one, two, or three columns. These are exactly what they sound like, with columns of content displayed vertically on the screen that contain the information of the blog. In a one-column layout, the blog posts are found in the single column, with secondary content being relegated to a header or footer, usually site navigation. In a two-column layout, there is normally a main column that holds the blog posts, with a secondary column, or sidebar, directly adjacent to the main column on the left side, or less frequently on the right. This column is used to hold secondary content for the blog: navigation, blogroll, link to the feed, or other content. This secondary column is a popular place for badges that show participation in other sites (Flickr, Twitter, or hundreds of others). In a three-column layout, you typically have a main column and two sidebars.

It is certainly possible to deviate significantly from a column-based layout for a blog, but it is worth starting slowly with a basic two-column layout for a library that is just starting to blog. You can always move to a more complicated template or theme once you have the basics down and feel comfortable.

Being native also means being more than just a marketing tool for your library. Blogs are voices, and we all know what a marketing voice sounds like today. Certainly use the blog to market yourself, but make sure that it's not all you do and that the blog has content that the patrons ask for instead of what you think they need. In a public library it's well worth promoting your story hours, but listing the top 10 staff picks might be more interesting to more people, because it shows the people behind the blog and allows their voice to shine through. For an academic library, posting your new books is a great way to make faculty happy, but a post about the best places in the library to find a quiet spot during finals is probably far more valuable to your students.

Take some time and browse the library blogosphere before you dive in. See how different libraries do things, and then make your library blog even better.

CHAPTER 13

# *Future Possibilities*

I n Chapter 11 we discussed the current ways in which libraries are using blogs today. But what might the library blogs of the future look like? The nature of blogs has changed so much in the last two years that it is difficult to say with great certainty what the library blogs of the future might look like. One thing is certain, throughout the Web, the nature of blogs are changing. So much so that the Pew Internet and American Life Project discovered when surveying Web users that many did not even realize that they were creating or consuming blogs. Much of this is due to the rise of social networking sites like Facebook and MySpace that allow users to create and consume "blogs" without knowing they are doing so.

Social networking sites such as MySpace and Facebook facilitate the communication and exchange of information among "friends." MySpace is a popular social networking site for teens that allows users to create personal profiles, blogs, groups, and networks of friends. Users can upload photos and video, in addition to the traditional features of social networking sites. MySpace allows users to create their own personal blog on which others can comment. MySpace allows users to post items to a "bulletin board" so that their friends can see. These two features give MySpace blog-like qualities that users can exploit.

Several libraries have developed MySpace profiles. The Brooklyn College Library deployed their MySpace profile in March of 2006. The profile is used to promote library events, collect user comments, and answer questions. In a 2006 Library Journal article, Beth Evans, who created the Brooklyn College Library's MySpace profile asserts, "Reading student profiles allows us to be a little playful with students and in some cases teach them about the library without their even asking for such information." Because users voluntarily put a lot of information about themselves in MySpace and choose to share it with their "friends," a library can use this information to learn more about users who have "friended" them.

Hennepin County Library in Minnesota also uses MySpace to interact with its users and uses the blog portion in particular to post about upcoming events <http://www.myspace.com/hennepincountylibrary>. Additionally, Hennepin County Library uses the Pictures feature of MySpace as a mini-photo blog. One outstanding feature of the Hennepin County Library's MySpace profile is the links back to the library's Web site. The profile contains a search box for the library catalog, links to new books, music, and movies as well as a MySpace group specifically set up by the library.

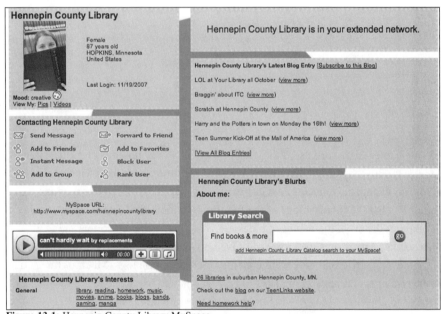

**Figure 13-1:** Hennepin County Library MySpace

Because a significant number of MySpace users are teens, this service is likely more relevant for public and school libraries than academic libraries. However, some academic libraries have ventured into MySpace. The University of Texas has a good MySpace profile <http://www.myspace.com/utlibraries>. This library uses the blog feature to post news and events. This library's profile also contains excellent links back to the library Web site including links to tutorials on how to find a book, information on electronic books, links to the media collections, and the Ask a Librarian service.

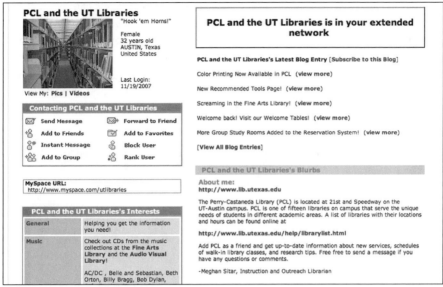

**Figure 13-2:** University of Texas Austin Undergraduate Library MySpace

MySpace groups also offer outreach opportunities for librarians. In particular, academic librarians with discipline-specific instruction and collection-development responsibilities could use MySpace groups to interact with students in their particular discipline.

Another social networking tool is Facebook. Started by a student at Harvard University, Facebook provides similar services and features as MySpace. However, it is more popular with college students. Many aspects of Facebook mimic the function of traditional blogs. For example, Facebook's posted items allow Facebook users to post items of interest: links, videos, music, etc., to their friends. Friends can then comment on the items posted. Facebook users have a "wall" to which they can add text posts for their friends to read. In many ways, these features are very similar to blogging since many bloggers post both text and items of interest to their blogs and readers can comment on these.

Many academic libraries are currently exploring and experimenting with Facebook because of the high number of college students using the service. One way in which libraries might consider using Facebook is for subject liaisons to interface with a specific class or department via a Facebook group. The librarian could use the blog-like aspects of Facebook to deliver specific information to this targeted user group. Some have questioned the value of libraries having this type of presence in social networking tools, but in some cases, this seems valid. The 2007-2008 first year law students at the University of Houston Law Center have a Facebook group. Librarians at the Law Library might use this group to target helpful library information to these students.

To create a presence in Facebook, libraries need to create a Facebook page either for itself or a Facebook group, both of which are slightly different from creating a profile on Facebook. Facebook pages have similar features to profiles, but a page has fans instead of friends. Unlike friends in Facebook, pages cannot see the profiles of their fans. However, one advantage of Facebook pages is that they can have several administrators, which make them easier for a library to distribute management. Note that in order to visit any of the Facebook URLs mentioned in the next several paragraphs, you must have an account and be logged into Facebook.

One interesting Facebook page created by a library is the page of the Wendt Library at the University of Wisconsin-Madison <http://www.facebook.com/profile.php?id=5593804617>.

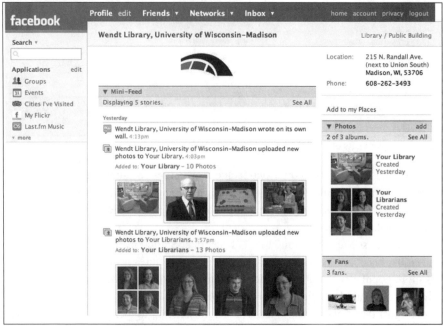

**Figure 13-3:** University of Wisconsin at Madison Library's Facebook

This library uses Facebook to post news, events, and links to important information. The library has created three albums that function similar to photo blogs. One album is entitled Your Library and features photos of the library and activities going on there. Another album is called Your Librarians and features photos of librarians. The last album is Your Resources + Services and features images related to important resources that the library offers such as Engineering Village, RefWorks, and IEE Xplore. This album allows the library to effectively market their services to students, faculty, and staff.

Public libraries also have established a presence in Facebook.

**Figure 13-4:** Photos on University of Wisconsin at Madison Library's Facebook

The Ottawa Public Library uses the "wall" feature of Facebook to post news, events, and information <http://www.facebook.com/group.php?gid=2376591023> ). They also use the photo feature of Facebook to post photos from events and programming at the library. They use Facebook's event feature to post upcoming library events.

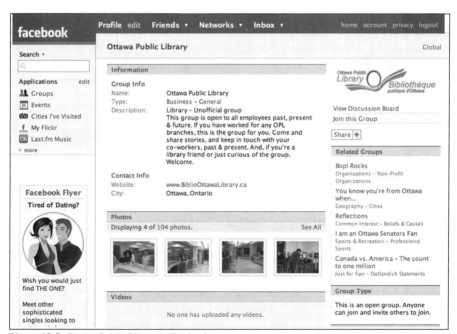

**Figure 13-5:** Ottawa Public Library's Facebook

Other libraries have created Facebook groups. One advantage of Facebook groups over Facebook pages is that people who join automatically receive updates from that group while users who become a "fan" can choose if they receive updates. Both pages and groups appear as part of a profile of people who have joined the group or "fanned" the page, thus enabling your library to be found by other people via their social network. Like pages, groups can have multiple administrators.

The Lester Public Library created a Facebook group for its users <http://www.facebook.com/group.php?gid=5540830842>, and the University of Massachusetts at Amherst Libraries has created a group for graduate students interested in information about the libraries <http://www.facebook.com/group.php?gid=14266705084&ref=nf>. Facebook Groups seem to be a viable option for Groups related to the library, such as Friends of the Library groups.

Another interesting phenomenon developing in the blogging world at large is the idea of microblogging. Sites like Twitter and Jaiku allow users to create compact posts about what is going on in their lives. Facebook and MySpace also include microblogging in the form of the "my status" section of a user's profile. Typically, microblogging is used for brief status updates rather than longer posts. Several libraries are using microblogging to push out short advertisements and news to students, faculty, and staff. The University of Illinois at Urbana-Champaign uses its Twitter account in this manner <http://twitter.com/askundergrad>. Microposts on the status of the catalog, the upcoming gaming night, and how to get help on your research paper provide undergraduate students with timely information. The Cleveland Public Library uses Twitter in a very similar manner, posting information about author Sherman Alexie's appearance, new resources like Naxos Music Library, and events like citizenship classes <http://twitter.com/Cleveland_PL>.

Other libraries are exploring the idea of microblogging for reference. The Nebraska Library Commission has posted its reference questions using Twitter <http://twitter.com/NLC_Reference>. The AskUsNow! Service, which allows Maryland state residents, students, and workers to get round-the-clock help from a librarian online, also uses Twitter to post online reference questions <http://twitter.com/askusnow>. Once a question is posted it is also available via the "currently being asked" section of the internal AskUsNow! staff Web site.

This use of microblogging helps reference librarians and staff stay aware of what questions are currently being asked by their users. It could be taken to another level if both the question and the answer were posted allowing library users to leverage questions currently being asked as well.

Reference questions, news, and events aren't the only uses for microblogging. Recent additions from the library catalog or federated search tool are also potential content for a microblog. Dave Pattern has been experimenting with this idea at the University of Huddersfield (UK). While the development of microblogging allows libraries to post compact tidbits, other changes in blogging are enabling libraries to run their entire Web sites from a blog.

Many blogging platforms such as WordPress and Movable Type are moving towards becoming true content management systems that libraries could use to manage their whole Web site. Scriblio (formerly WPopac), developed by Casey Bisson of

Plymouth State University Library and originally based on the WordPress blogging software, is one example of blogging software becoming a content management system. Scriblio started out as the idea of taking the content of the library catalog and presenting it in a blog. Since the project began in 2006 as WPopac, the system has evolved from catalog as a blog to a full-featured content management system capable of managing many different kinds of content from physical resources to digital objects such as photos.

**Figure 13-6:** Scriblio at Plymouth State University Library

Using a blog in place of the traditional OPAC to show books to library users has several distinct advantages. The most important is that library users can add comments to records. This is something that, until very recently, was not available in any library catalog. Scriblio also puts all the relevant information about an object—title, author, description and reviews, availability, subject and related objects—onto a single screen. Additionally, items in Scriblio have tags, faceted browsing, book jackets, and links to other resources. Another distinct advantage of Scriblio is that it contains a built-in RSS feed. This means that a library user can subscribe to the feed and see all new items the library has acquired along with news and other important information.

**Figure 13-7:** Scriblio RSS Feed

Scriblio isn't just being used to power the Plymouth State University Library Web site. It also powers the Tamworth, New Hampshire public library (Cook Memorial Library) Web site. Like the Plymouth State University Library Web site, the Cook Memorial Library Web site features tags and book jackets. Scriblio provides its users with information about new books and new videos in an easily browseable format.

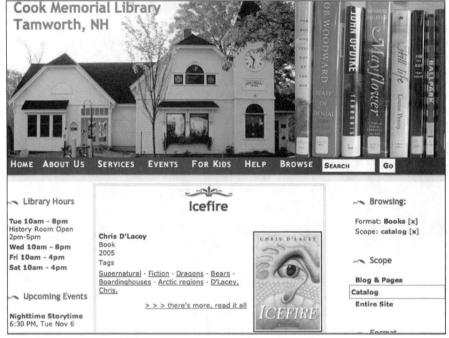

**Figure 13-8:** Cook Memorial Public Library

This merging of blog and content management system is not a unique phenomenon. Ann Arbor District Library uses Drupal, an open source content management system, to power its Web site. While this may not seem significant, the basic components of Drupal are very similar to a blog. Most pages within Drupal allow users to comment on them. Moreover, a feed of changes to the Web site can be created from Drupal.

Blog-like content management systems and extended blog software aside, an entire Web site can easily be built using either WordPress or Movable Type. Both of these blogging platforms offer the pages feature that allows libraries to create content that is non-chronological in nature. The main challenge with using either of these systems as a content management system is altering the code so that the first page a user sees doesn't have to be a reverse chronological listing of posts.

In pre-2.1 versions of WordPress, this meant editing the Main Index Template (index.php) to look like the home page you wanted. To do this, you needed a moderate understanding of HTML and PHP. However, as of WordPress Version 2.1, you can set any page as the home page for your site by going to Options > Reading, changing Front Page display to a static page, and selecting the page you want displayed from the drop-down menu.

**Figure 13-9:** WordPress Reading Options

This functionality makes WordPress very close to a true content management system. Like the server-based version of WordPress available at WordPress.org, WordPress.com also offers the ability to change the homepage to be an existing page within WordPress. As a result, one could use a WordPress.com account to create and manage an entire Web site.

Movable Type also offers enough to be used as a content management system for a library Web site. To alter the home page, though, you have to edit the Main Index Template so that it looks like a traditional Web page rather than a reverse chronological listing of posts. To do this you need knowledge of HTML and Movable Type tags. Unlike WordPress, there doesn't appear to be a simple way to tell Movable Type that you want an existing page to be your home page. This makes Movable Type slightly more difficult to use as a content management system. However, Movable Type has other features, such as strong media management, that may make it desirable as a content management system. Of all the blogging software we reviewed in this book, Blogger is the only one that isn't capable of being used as a content management system. This is because it does not provide a pages feature that would allow users to create content outside the scope of posts.

As you can see, the idea of using blogging software to run an entire library Web site isn't far-fetched. For smaller libraries with limited staff and resources, blogging software might be a viable option to creating a dynamic and interactive virtual presence that can be easily maintained.

Because of their strength in providing an interface to easily create, edit and maintain content, blogs are also increasingly becoming repositories for media, whether it be born digital content or digitized materials. In Chapter 10 we discussed the idea of podcasting, photoblogs, and videoblogs. With the rise of YouTube, Flickr, and other media-sharing services, multimedia is becoming an increasingly important part of the Internet and as a result, blogs.

Several libraries have noted this trend and have experimented with using blogs to provide access to their digital collections. What makes blogging software good for managing digital collections is that blogs allow users to interact with and provide feedback on these collections. Two excellent examples of blogs being used to manage digital collections are the Beyond Brown Paper exhibit powered by Scriblio and created by the library and Plymouth State University <http://beyondbrownpaper.plymouth.edu/> and the Western Springs History exhibit <http://www. westernspringshistory.org/>. Both of these digital library projects exploit the power of blogs by allowing users to comment and tag items within the collection.

Beyond Brown Paper is an archive of photos from the Brown Manufacturing Company in northern New Hampshire. This site contains historical photographs that date from the late 19th century through the mid-1960s.

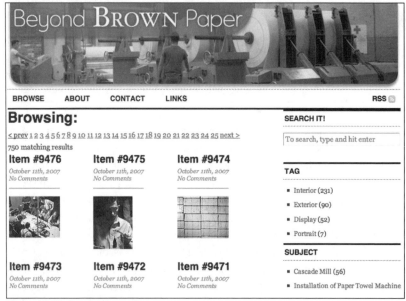

**Figure 13-10:** Beyond Brown Paper

What is fabulous about putting digital collections in a blog-like system is that library users can comment on collections. In the case of this collection, many users comment on the photographs providing important historical details such as information about the photo's location or people in the photo. This project leverages the power of the user-contributed information to enhance metadata about digital objects. This is a feature most digital library systems do not currently offer.

---

**1 RESPONSE SO FAR ↓**

**Leo J. Belanger** // Nov 4, 2007 at 3:40 pm

The first tall indiv on the left is Bob Lowe, he was our swimming instructor, and basketball coach during that period and was a great man. He was there until i went into the Army in 1958.

---

**Figure 13-11:** Commented Digital Object at Beyond Brown Paper

Western Springs Public Library's Western Spring History Blog <http://www.westernspringshistory.org/> is one part historical exhibit and one part digital repository. It contains historical photos of Western Springs, Illinois, complete with metadata, which have been entered as tags.

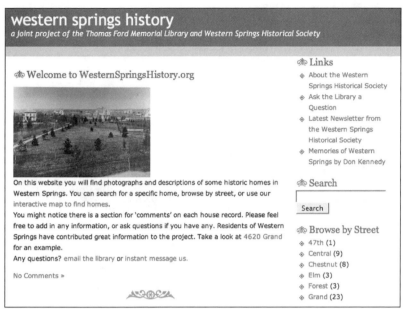

**Figure 13-12:** Western Springs History

Other homegrown digital library systems are incorporating many aspects of blogs to the point that they are becoming very blog-like in nature. For example, the Great Lakes Images collection <http://www.hhpl.on.ca/GreatLakes/GLImages/> allows users to comment on images that are part of the collection.

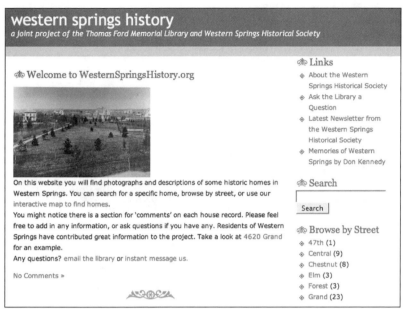

**Figure 13-13:** Example Comment from Great Lakes Images Web Site

Comments are particularly useful with digital library materials because they can be used to leverage user knowledge to improve descriptions of images and the collection.

Additionally, some libraries are using Flickr to highlight their digital collections. The Combined Arms Research Library uses Flickr for its digital library collections

<http://www.flickr.com/photos/59804400@N00/>. Not only does this give librarians access to tagging and comments, but it also creates a photoblog for the collection.

**Figure 13-14:** Combined Arms Research Library Flickr Photoblog

The Redwood City Public Library is also using Flickr in this way <http://www.flickr.com/photos/redwoodcitylibrary/sets/72157600508615810/>. By using Flickr these libraries have a psuedo-photoblog to which library users can sub-scribe, add comments, and track content as it is added.

Even though blogging may be changing dramatically, it can still serve many useful and important purposes to libraries. Whether it be providing access to news or digital collections, managing the library Web site, facilitating internal communi-cations, or gathering feedback on a building project, blogs are versatile and adaptable tools that are helping non-technically savvy people interact with and make content available to a wider audience.

**Figure 13-15:** Redwood City History Flickr Photoblog

# SUMMARY

After exploring the use of blogs in libraries, we hope that you are excited about the potential that blogging can bring to your library and the problems that a blog might solve for you. While there is no one-size-fits-all solution for blogging, especially in libraries, the variety of platforms and options in this book are designed to give you enough familiarity to be comfortable trying a blog on for size and seeing how it fits your library.

There are innumerable things that could get in the way of implementation of a blog at your library, even if you believe it's the right tool for the job. Touchy IT departments that are more concerned with security than service, frightened administrators who fear the public's reaction if anything untoward is posted in the comments and apathetic faculty and staff who just aren't interested in new tools—all of these exist in some form in libraries. If that is the case for you, try showing the questioning person some of the examples we've described. Get them online and show them the conversation. Try to put them in a position so they can see how powerful it can be when you include the patrons you are serving in the conversation. In 10 years, who knows if we'll still be talking about blogs; we guarantee that libraries will still be talking about including patrons in the conversation.

We've tried to give examples of as many different types of library blogs as we could imagine, but in any print source you can't include everything. Print has limitations that electronic sources simply don't have, including lead times for publication. Luckily, we have the Internet at our disposal and consequently have created a Web site to go along with the book that has links to library blogs we find interesting and occasional posts on blogs and blogging in libraries. That Web site can be found at: <http://www.libraryblogging.com>

Join us there to get updates, chat with the authors, and find information about libraries and blogging.

The individual tools aren't the most important part of this book, even though we've spent the majority of the pages walking through them. Each tool, whether hosted or installed, free or paid, open or closed, has at its core the ability to give a voice to a person or group. By giving voice, these tools invite disagreement, they invite confirmation, they invite people to question that voice. All blogs are, in effect, an individual or individuals that want to be heard, pushing their voice out over the Internet and hoping that someone wants to listen. The secret is, if you find interesting things to say, lots of people will listen, including your patrons.

Grab a blog, and join the conversation!

# APPENDIX

## *Blogging Tools*

**Blogger** - <http://www.blogger.com>

**Class Blogmeister** - <http://www.classblogmeister.com>

**Drupal** - <http://www.drupal.org>

**Edublogs** - <http://www.edublogs.org>

**LiveJournal** - <http://www.livejournal.com>

**Lyceum** - <http://lyceum.ibiblio.org>

**MovableType** - <http://www.movabletype.com>

**MySpace** - <http://www.myspace.com>

**Subtext** (<http://subtextproject.com/>)

**Textpattern** - <http://www.textpattern.com>

**TypePad** – <http://www.typepad.com>

**Typo** - <http://typosphere.org/>

**Windows Live Spaces™** - <http://spaces.live.com>

**WordPress.com** - <http://www.wordpress.com>

**WordPress** - <http://www.wordpress.org>

**WordPress MU** - <http://mu.wordpress.org>

# GLOSSARY

**Atom** - Two standards, one is in an XML format for syndication and the other is a publishing protocol that allows blog owners to publish a "feed" of recent posts or content in standardized, machine-readable format. The feed can then be used by other Web sites or subscribed to by Internet users via a feed reader program.

**Blogger** - A popular Web-based blog publishing service that is owned by Google.

**Blogosphere** – The collective noun for groups of blogs. Often seen with a limiting descriptor, a.k.a "the library blogosphere."

**Comments** - A feature in blogs that allow readers to add responses to posts.

**Creative Commons** - A non-profit organization that is devoted to enabling copyright holders to grant some or all of their rights to the public while retaining others through a variety of licensing and contract schemes. The organization has created and released several copyright licenses known as Creative Commons licenses that restrict only certain rights (or none) of a work. Blog creators can choose to apply a particular Creative Commons license to their blog.

**CSS** – Cascading Style Sheet. CSS is normally used to provide the design/user interface of a blog, separate from the content/information, which is normally HTML or XHTML.

**Enclosure** - Non-text files which are attached to feed items.

**Facebook** - A social networking Web site that allows people to communicate and exchange information with friends.

**Feedburner** - A news feed management service that assists bloggers with creating customized feed for their blogs and provides tools for managing feeds and analyzing feed traffic.

**Feed reader** - Also known as a feed aggregator or aggregator. A program for aggregating syndicated Web content such as news headlines, blogs, and podcasts and presenting that content to a user in a consumable manner.

**Folksonomy** – The informational taxonomy created by a collection of tagged objects.

**LiveJournal** - A virtual community where Internet users can keep a blog. Unlike other blog publishing services, LiveJournal has more of a community feel and offers some features similar to social networking software such as MySpace.

**Mashup** - A Web site or application that combines data from more than one source.

**MovableType** - An open source, Web-based blog publishing platform capable of supporting multiple blogs, which is written with PHP and can have a backend database of MySQL, Berkeley DB, PostgreSQL, and SQLite.

**MP3** - MPEG Level 3; an open standard for the creation of digital audio files.

**MySpace** - A social networking Web site that allows users to create personal profiles, networks of friends, groups, and blogs and share photos, music, and video.

**Photoblog** - A blog that is predominantly used to publish and share photos rather than text.

**Plugin** - A small piece of software that adds on functionality to an existing blog publishing system.

**Podcast** - A set of media files that are distributed over the Internet using syndication (RSS or Atom) and can be subscribed to using a feed reader or podcast reader, so that new content is automatically downloaded when it is added.

**RSS** - A set of XML formats that allow blog owners to publish a "feed" of recent posts or content in standardized, machine-readable format. The feed can then be used by other Web sites or subscribed to by Internet users via a feed reader program.

**Sidebar** - The smaller column or columns in a multiple-column layout for a blog. The sidebar is often referred to by its location: "the right sidebar is having problems."

**Social Networking Software** - Software that allows users to build online social networks of people who share interests and activities.

**Tags** - A keyword or other relevant term assigned to an object, typically a blog post when used in connection with blogs, which provides descriptive information about the object and enables searching and classification. Tags of blog posts are typically chosen by the person creating the post.

**Theme** - The "look and feel" of a weblog. Blogger refers to these as templates. Themes are normally CSS-based.

**Trackback** - A method for blog authors to request notification when someone links to one of their posts. This technology allows blog authors to keep track of who is linking and referring to their content.

**Videoblog** - A blog that is predominantly used to publish and share videos.

**WordPress** - A free, open source, Web-based blogging platform written in PHP and using MySQL for the backend database. WordPress is available in two varieties: single blog or a multi-blog variant called Wordpress MU.

**WYSIWYG Editor** - What You See Is What You Get Editor; an editor that displays what you are entering exactly as you will see it when the information has been submitted and processed.

# INDEX

## A

Academic Libraries 13-16
    examples of 13-16, 114, 117-119
ACRLog 121-122
Ann Arbor District Library 17, 41-42, 140
Askimet 35, 43
AskUsNow! 138
Asset Management 38, 82
Atom 91-97
    See also Syndication
Austin Public Library 17-18

## B

Beyond Brown Paper 141-142
Blog as OPAC 138-140
Blog Culture 127-131
Blog roll
    See Blogroll
Bloglines 101,102
Blogs
    definition of 3
    for Academic Libraries
        See Academic Library Blogs
    for announcements
        See News
    for Conference Content
        See Conference Content
    for digital collections
        See Digital Collections
    for documentation 120-121
    for events
        See Events
    for external marketing
        See External Marketing
    for feedback 120
    for internal communication
        See Internal Communication
    for Library Organizations
        See Library Organization Blogs
    for new books
        See New Books
    for news
        See News
    for Public Libraries
        See Public Library Blogs
    for Reviews
        See Reviews
    for School Libraries
        See School Library Blogs
    for Specific User Groups
        examples of 112, 116
    history of 4-7
Blogroll 8, 18, 131

## Blogger

Blogger
    configuring 56-58
    Customizing Look and Feel 60-63
    FTP 63
    How to 55-64
    permissions 60
    posting 59
    templates 60, 62
Boston Regional Library System 124, 125
Brooklyn College Library 134
Business Blog 117

## C

Case Western University 39
Categories 7, 12, 13, 14, 21, 43, 71, 79, 86-87,
    91, 97, 102-103, 112, 120
Chicago-Ken College of Law Library 120
Class Blogmeister 31-32
Cleveland Public Library 138
Code of Conduct 129-30
Cohen, Steven 7
Colorado College Library 114
Columbus Public Library 18
Combined Arms Research Library 144
Comments 3-4, 7-8, 79, 82, 87, 90-91, 96, 97,
    113, 120, 128, 129, 134, 139, 143-144
    Blogger 59
    Movable Type 37, 72, 79
    spam 35, 37, 43, 72
    WordPress 35
    WordPress.com 44
Community Server 25
Conference Content 121, 122, 124
Content Management System 7, 15, 25, 33, 34,
    40, 41, 138-141
Cook Memorial Library 140
Creative Commons 109

## D

Darien Public Library 115-116
del.ico.us 98-105
Digital Collections 141-144
Dover Public Library 18-19
Drupal 25, 33, 41, 140

## E

Edublogs.org 31, 36
External Marketing 8, 13, 16, 19, 108, 135

## F

Facebook 135-138
Feed readers 101-102
    browser-integrated 102
    desktop 101

web-based 101-102
Feed2JS 101, 104
Feedburner 87, 98-101
    See also Syndication
FeedDemon 101
Firefox
    feed support 102
Flickr
    for photoblogging 106-107, 144

**G**

Gargoyles Loose in the Library 22
George Mason University Library 119-120
Georgia State University Library 113-114, 118-119
Google Reader 102, 105
GoogleVideo 49

**H**

Health Science Library at University at Buffalo 117-118
Hennepin County Public Library 134
Homer Township Public Library 116-117
Hosted Blogging Software 23-25, 27-32

**I**

Internal Communication 13, 119-121

**J**

Jaiku 138

**K**

Kansas State University Libraries 120-121
King, David Lee 108

**L**

Lansing Illinois Public Library 113-114
Lester Public Library 138
Levine, Jenny 8
Library Organization Blogs 121-125
LibraryStuff 7
LITABlog 108, 121-122
LiveJournal 4-5, 29-30
Lyceum 36, 40, 67

**M**

Madison-Jefferson County Public Library 41, 112-113
Mashups 104-106
Media Repositories 144-145
Michigan Library Consortia 121, 123-124
Microblogging 138
Mosman Library (Australia) 41
Movable Type 36-39, 71-83
    Customizing Look and Feel 80-82
    How to 71-83
    Installing 72-78
    media 38
    notifications 38

pages 79
permissions 38
plugins 37
roles 38
styles 80-81
templates 81
widgets 81-82
MySpace 133-135

**N**

Nebraska Library Commission 138
NetNewsWire 101
New Books
    examples of 112, 114, 115
News 12
    examples of 111-119
News Aggregators
    See Feed Readers
News Feeds
    See Syndication
NewsGator 101
North Carolina State University Library 118

**O**

Odeo 44, 45, 53-54
Ohio State University 18
Olson Middle School 21
Ottawa Public Library 137

**P**

Papercuts 19, 111-112
Permissions 35, 38
Photoblogging 106-107
    examples of 113-114, 142, 144
Photoblogs
    See Photoblogging
PLA Blog 122-123
Planet Code4Lib 105-106
Plymouth State University Library 138-139
Podcasting 107-108
    examples of 107, 121
Public Library Association Blog
    See PLA Blog
Public Library Blogs 16-20
    examples of 111-112, 112-113, 113-114,
      115-116, 134, 136-138, 140, 142-143, 144

**R**

Readers Advisory
    See Reviews
Real Simple Syndication
    See RSS
Redwood City Public Library 144
Reference 91, 99, 110-11
Regina Public Library 115
Reviews
    examples of 111, 115, 120, 139

Rich Site Syndication
See RSS
Roles
Movable Type 38
WordPress 35
Rojo 102
RSS 86-91
See also Syndication
Rundlett Middle School 21

## S

Safari
feed support 102
School Library Blogs 20-22, 31-32
Scriblio 138-140
Server-based blogging software 25-26, 33-42
Subject Blogs 117-119
Subtext 40
Syndication 85-97

## T

Tag Cloud 103-104
Tags
See Tagging
Tagging 102-104
Tamworth, NH Public Library
See Cook Memorial Library
Textpattern 25, 33, 41
The Shifted Librarian 7
Topeka-Shawnee Public Library 19-20, 108,
111-112
Trackback 4
Twitter 138
Typepad 28-29
Typo 40

## U

University Laboratory High School Library 22
University of British Columbia 39
University of Calgary 41
University of Houston Libraries 119
University of Illinois Champaign Urbana
Library 138
University of Massachusetts at Amherst
Libraries 138
University of Minnesota Libraries 39
University of North Carolina at Chapel Hill
Library 15
University of Prince Edward Island 41
University of Saskatchewan 39
University of Texas at Austin Library 134-135
University of Wisconsin-Madison Library 136
UThink 39

## V

Videoblogging 108
Virginia Tech Library 15

## W

Wake Forest University 120
Web-based aggregators 101-102
Web-based blog services
See Hosted Blogging Software
Weblog
see Blog
Wendt Library
See University of Wisconsin-Madison Library
Western Kentucky University Library 15
Western Springs History Exhibit 141, 143
Western Springs Public Library 141, 143
Windows Live Spaces 32
Wisconsin Library Association 124
WordPress
How to 65-69
plugins 69
themes 68
WordPress.org
See WordPress
WordPress.com 30, 43-54
audio 53
configuring 44-47
Customizing Look and Feel 47-49
How to 43-54
photos 49-51
posting 49-54
themes 47
video 51-53
widgets 48
WordPressMU 36, 67

## Y

YouTube 35, 44, 49, 51-53, 106, 141